CRACKING THE COVER

A BEGINNER'S GUIDE TO THE BIBLE

Gary Sharpe '98

CRACKING THE COVER

A BEGINNER'S GUIDE TO THE BIBLE

ROSS L. SMILLIE

UNITED CHURCH PUBLISHING HOUSE
Toronto, Ontario

Cracking the Cover
A Guide to Biblical Literacy

Canadian Cataloguing in Publication Data

Smillie, Ross L. (Ross Lawrence), 1959-
        Cracking the cover : a user's guide to the Bible

Includes bibliographical references.
ISBN 1-55134-069-0

1. Bible - Introductions.   I. Title.

BS475.2.S64 1997   220.6'1   C97-930498-9

The United Church Publishing House
3250 Bloor Street West
Etobicoke, Ontario, Canada
M8X 2Y4
416-231-5931
bookpub@uccan.org

Printed in Canada
5 4 3 2 1   02 01 00 99 98

Design and production: Department of Publications and Graphics

970137 ♲

Dedication

To my parents, Doreen and Larry Smillie, my wife, Therese Thompson, and my children, Sara and Sean, who surround me with love and faithfulness.

DEDICATION

Contents

CONTENTS

This book was written as part of a project to develop biblical literacy undertaken by the Evangelization and Discipleship Committee of the Alberta and Northwest Conference, The United Church of Canada. The committee sought to understand why more and more church members are not learning to read the Bible.

One hunch was that the church does not challenge such people with clear, attainable goals. In response the committee developed a list of such goals. That list was adopted by the 1993 Annual Meeting of Alberta and Northwest Conference as a primary goal for all members and adherents, and particularly for new members and adherents.

The committee felt the need for a short, inexpensive, and easily accessible resource that could introduce people to each of these goals. This book was written to fulfil that need. Each chapter explains the meaning of one of the goals and provides exercises that will help the reader digest and integrate the material. Readings from a variety of ecumenical and historical sources are included to help people begin to develop experience in reading and interpreting the Bible.

Introductions to the Bible are not new. They have been produced at many stages of the church's history. They have ranged from short catechisms to major theological works. Today, there are a wide variety of resources available to assist the church in its reading of scripture. Many of these resources are mentioned in chapter three.

This modest offering is presented in the hope that it can bring together in one short book resources that will help Christian disciples develop the basic skills and knowledge necessary to make fullest use of this strange and wonderful book that is at the heart of the church's life.

This book is not mine alone. I am grateful to the members of the Evangelization and Discipleship Committee from 1977 to 1993 who were a big part of the initial impetus for this book. I owe a special debt of gratitude to Rev. David Holmes, who used earlier drafts in newcomer groups at Robert McClure Memorial United Church in Calgary, and offered constructive suggestions and much-needed encouragement. Linda Gow, Mark Green, participants in workshops at Conference Annual Meetings, and the volunteer reviewers from the United Church Publishing House read drafts of the manuscript and offered valuable feedback. Margaret Woodrow has spent many hours in front of a photocopier making sure that drafts of this book were available for people to read and comment on. Margaret and Howard Woodrow, Irene Aasen, Evelyn Fretwell, Terry Maetche, Leanne Benoit, and Joan Meeres participated in a final "test run" group study and had valuable insights. Thanks also to the people of Ardmore United Church, St. John's United Church in Bonnyville, Southminster-Steinhauer United Church in Edmonton, and St. Andrew's United Church in Lacombe, for their enthusiasm for the faith, courage in asking questions, and willingness to be guinea pigs in a young minister's experiments in adult Christian education.

Writing a book like this is a humbling experience. In the face of a subject as vast and wonderful as the Bible there is always more that could have been said, perhaps should have been said, and more that should have been said differently. Compared to the grandeur of the subject, I am painfully aware of my own inadequacies. But in view of the crying need for such resources, I am convinced that the effort, however inadequate, is worth making. It is my hope that this book will help many people to take the first step on the lifelong journey into the strange and wonderful world of the Bible.

Introduction

When I was in elementary school, two men from an organization called the Gideons came to my school and offered every one of the hundred or so grade five students a small copy of the New Testament and Psalms. Their only condition for this free gift was that we promise to read a little bit of it every day. The vast majority of the students accepted their New Testament, along with that commitment. I don't know what everyone else was thinking, but I had no intention of reading it every day. But, since everyone else was taking one, I saw no reason not to. So I took my Testament, brought it home, looked at it a couple of times, and then put it in a drawer somewhere.

But that promise kept nagging at me, along with a sense of curiosity about this book that these Gideons, whoever they were, considered so important that they were willing to give hundreds of them away so freely, like casting seeds to the wind, with no way of knowing whether their efforts would bear fruit.

So every couple of years, I would pick that little book up again and try to read it. Some of the stories and sayings I had heard before in church, but many of the others were unfamiliar and strange. It was a hard book to read, but as hard as it was, the stories had an odd power, a way of cropping up in my memory at peculiar times. I found myself encountering situations that, even though they were quite different from those in the Bible, reminded me of those stories and spoke to me of ways I might become a different and better person.

Still, I found it hard to read, and for many years I would periodically promise myself that I would read it regularly, but found that my resolution would only last a week or so. Attending Sunday school at my family's church wasn't much help. We learned the stories and talked a little about what they meant, but that didn't make it any easier to read. When I became a young adult I started to read some more detailed scholarship. That helped me understand some of the reasons why the Bible is so difficult to read, and I began to read the book in a new way. It was only once I understood what the book was and how it came to be that I really felt confident in reading it.

I came to recognize that the Bible is hard to read for some very good reasons. It is a collection of writings from an ancient culture and a faraway land, using languages that are no longer spoken anywhere, and referring to customs many of which have long since passed away. It uses many different literary genres: prayer, commandment, story, and proverb, to name a few. It speaks of events from the beginning of the world to a future judgement and "kingdom of God" in ways that are unfamiliar to modern ears. It includes stories of miraculous healings and events that are difficult for those of us trained in scientific ways of thinking about the world to believe. It has different accounts of the same events, and, often, the details of these accounts contradict each other. Finally, it has no obvious organization and there are odd disjunctions and shifts in style, language, and topic.

And yet, in spite of all these difficulties, the church dares to claim that it is through this book that we come to know God and to live as Christ's disciples. The Bible is read in church; it is quoted in sermons, Sunday school classes, and church documents of all kinds. It influences the things the church tries to encourage and the things we resist. Because of the Bible's importance in the church it has become an important cultural document, and knowledge of its contents is essential to understanding the history and literature of the western world.

Faced with both the bewildering complexity of the Bible and its singular importance, you may feel stuck. You may want to explore this book but may be unsure of when or how to get started.

In the pages that follow, you will explore what it means to be *biblically literate*. Literacy refers to the ability to read with understanding; biblical literacy means to be able to read the Bible with understanding. A literate person does not need to know everything, but being literate means that we have access to the vast store of information, insight, and entertainment that are available to someone who can read. In the same way, to be biblically literate does not mean to know everything about the Bible, but to know just enough to make the rest available.

Reading the Bible can be compared to baking a loaf of bread. If you've never baked one before or, if every time you've tried, you've come out with something inedible, you might be leaving out one of the main ingredients. It helps to have a recipe. Think of what follows as a recipe for biblical literacy.

There are nine basic ingredients to biblical literacy, each of which is explored in one of the nine chapters of this book. Just as a bread recipe includes many different kinds of ingredients, so this recipe includes a variety of attitudes, knowledge, experiences, abilities, and imagination:

- an attitude of openness to the leading of God's Spirit;

- a knowledge of the basic story of the Bible;

- an ability to use some basic tools for Bible study;

- an understanding of some key words and figures of speech;

- an ability to recognize different types of literature;

- an understanding of how the Bible came into being;

- a sensitivity to the differences between the biblical world and our own;

- some experience with how the Bible is read by people of other places and times;

- creative imagination to make the connections between the Bible and our own lives.

If these ingredients seem intimidating, don't despair! Remember that to be biblically literate, you need only have a little dash of each. Then you will have the basic ingredients for a lifetime of exploration.

It is also much like getting ready to go camping for the first time. You have to have some basic equipment and the knowledge of what to do with it. Once you've got that, you just have to get started. And after your first twenty-four hours in camp, you'll be a lot more confident.

These ingredients are all important. Each of the chapters of this book will train you in using one of the ingredients. This training is an active process, so each chapter includes exercises designed to involve you in what you learn. Most of us learn best by doing, rather than just by reading, so I encourage you not to skip the exercises.

After each chapter, there is a reading about a specific biblical text. You may well find these readings the most interesting part of the book. They are intended to supplement chapters eight and nine by giving you some experience in reading the Bible, hearing what people of other places and times have said about it, and applying it to your own lives. The readings are only a small sample of the vast amount of writing on the Bible from many different times and places. Although I have tried to find interesting readings from various places and times, I do not claim that they are representative. But they will get you started. To get the maximum benefit from these selections, read the introduction, then read the Bible passage on which the selection is based. Then read the selection and think about the questions that follow. Space is provided for you to write your answers, but if you need additional room, you may find it helpful to record your answers on another piece of paper or in a journal.

I have arranged the chapters and readings in an order that to me seems to proceed logically, but you may find yourself wanting to explore them in a different order depending on your own background and experience. This is a workbook, so work your way through it in a way that suits your own needs. And don't be afraid to write in it, either in the margins or the spaces provided for that purpose.

Each of the chapters and readings is short enough to be read at a single sitting, but some of them may require some pondering. If you find a chapter difficult on first reading, then read it again, do the exercises carefully, and, if you are still having difficulty, talk to a friend or a minister about what you have read. The Bible is a book that requires the use of creativity and imagination. Take the time to allow what you read to percolate and engage your imagination. You may find that drawing, sculpting, creative writing, or some other form of artistic expression may engage your imagination.

ONE

ONE

Why Read the Bible?

Someone once criticized a well-known preacher saying "I have been through the Bible forty times, and I have never found what you have been preaching." The preacher replied, "That may easily happen. What makes the difference is not how many times you have been through the Bible, but how many times and how thoroughly the Bible has been through you."[1]

That illustrates an important point about why we read the Bible. It is possible to read the Bible primarily out of an academic interest in ancient near eastern culture, literature, or history. There are many scholars who do just that. The Bible can also be read by those who want to find a religious blessing for beliefs, practices, or prejudices based primarily on other sources. But for disciples of Jesus throughout history, reading the Bible is primarily a spiritual activity. It is an effort to learn about God and to allow our lives to be shaped by the God we meet in the Bible. We read the Bible in the hope that God's Spirit will bless us and change us.

One of the most important passages in the Bible is in Paul's letter to the Christians in Rome. Paul wrote:

> *I appeal to you therefore, brothers and sisters, by the mercies of God, to present your bodies as a living sacrifice, holy and acceptable to God, which is your spiritual worship. Do not be conformed to this world, but be transformed by the renewing of your minds, so that you may discern what is the will of God — what is good and acceptable and perfect.*
>
> (Romans 12:1–2)

That passage expresses very well why we read the Bible: we read it in order to know who God is and what God wants, and to allow that knowledge to transform us.

In the church we read the Bible to learn about God. We think of the words of the Bible as *witnesses* to God. A witness in a court of law is someone who has witnessed (seen or heard) something, and is prepared to bear witness (testify) to it. It is the same with the Bible; human authors who have some experience of what God is doing in their lives, their communities, and their history have put pen to parchment and testified to that experience. In their testimony they point to God. They have witnessed something; now they bear witness to it.

Dietrich Bonhoeffer, a German pastor who was arrested and eventually executed for his opposition to the Nazis during World War II, once wrote that the Bible's "words and statements are not themselves true and eternal and holy, but only insofar as they bear witness to Christ." [2]

By bearing witness to God and to Christ, the Bible makes it possible for us to know God. This is why many churches use the ambiguous phrase "The Word of God" to refer to the Bible. Just as "love of God" can mean either "our love for God" or "God's love for us," so "Word of God" can mean either "a word about God" or "a word from God." The experience of people of faith is that it means both. For in the human testimony about God, we can experience God speaking to us.

This does not mean that the words of the Bible can be taken as the direct speech or dictation of God, as some people believe. Experiencing God speaking through these human words does not happen automatically, but remains a mysterious gift of God's Spirit. The words of the Bible remain human words, but sometimes in the act of reading what some people wrote about God many centuries ago, we actually encounter God guiding us in the present.

It is not only in reading the Bible that we meet God, for God is present all around us. We can experience God's presence in nature, in other people, and in ourselves. But it is often not easy to distinguish what is of God and what is not. The Bible helps us to sort that out. As John Calvin suggested, the Bible is like a pair of eyeglasses that helps us to see God's presence in the world around us. The difficult part is not to experience God's presence, but to recognize it when it happens.

What we learn about God through the Bible we apply to our own lives. Through meditation, prayer, imagination, and discussion we can bridge the distance between the biblical witness and our own lives, and learn what God is doing today and what God wants us to do. This is what most preachers try to do in their sermons. But in the same way that having a good doctor is no substitute for knowing what can make and keep you healthy, listening to a good preacher is no substitute for learning how to read the Bible.

Before we can bridge the distance between the world of the Bible and our own, however, we must first seek to understand as fully as possible what those people of ancient times were saying in their words about God. Because they wrote so long ago and belonged to such different cultures, it is easy to misunderstand what they were saying or to assume that what they were saying can be transferred directly to our own situation. Many of the other ingredients in this recipe for biblical literacy involve learning how to minimize the danger of this misunderstanding.

Exercises

Think carefully about each of these questions, write your answers below, and then discuss them with at least one other person.

1. In the course of your life what, if anything, have you been taught about the Bible?

2. In the teaching you received, was the emphasis placed on God speaking through the Bible or was it placed on the Bible as a human document?

3. Think of a time in your own life when you have had a sense of God's presence through something quite ordinary. Why do you think of it as God's presence?

4. What difference does it make to your understanding of God to encounter the sacred in the midst of the ordinary?

5. Think of a time in your life when you have misunderstood someone else because you assumed he or she was more like you than he or she was. How did you figure out that you misunderstood that person? Did you ever come to a fuller understanding?

One of the most important forms of biblical interpretation is the sermon. A sermon is an interpretation of a biblical text for a community of faith in a particular time and place. This sermon is by Martin Luther King, Jr., an American who came to international attention because of his leadership of the civil rights movement, a non-violent movement to challenge the laws and practices that segregated and impoverished African-Americans. A Baptist pastor with a doctorate in theology and deep roots in the black church, he was an inspiring speaker and leader. He was assassinated in 1968. This sermon articulates very effectively his combination of radical defiance of injustice with uncompromising commitment to nonviolence.

Transformed Nonconformist

Martin Luther King, Jr. (1929–68)

> *Be not conformed to this world: but be ye transformed by the renewing of your mind.*
>
> (Romans 12:2)

"Do not conform" is difficult advice in a generation when crowd pressures have unconsciously conditioned our minds and feet to move to the rhythmic drumbeat of the status quo. Many voices and forces urge us to choose the path of least resistance, and bid us never to fight for an unpopular cause and never to be found in a pathetic minority of two or three....

SECTION I

In spite of this prevailing tendency to conform, we as Christians have a mandate to be nonconformists. The Apostle Paul, who knew the inner realities of the Christian faith, counselled, "Be not conformed to this world: but be ye transformed by the renewing of your mind." We are called to be people of conviction, not conformity; of moral nobility, not social respectability. We are commanded to live differently and according to a higher loyalty....

This command not to conform comes, not only from Paul, but also from our Lord and Master, Jesus Christ, the world's most dedicated nonconformist, whose ethical nonconformity still challenges the conscience of mankind.

When an affluent society would coax us to believe that happiness consists in the size of our automobiles, the impressiveness of our houses, and the expensiveness of our clothes, Jesus reminds us, "A man's life consisteth not in the abundance of the things which he possesseth."

When we would yield to the temptation of a world rife with sexual promiscuity and gone wild with a philosophy of self-expression, Jesus tells us that "whosoever looketh on a woman to lust after her hath committed adultery with her already in his heart." ...

When we, through compassionless detachment and arrogant individualism, fail to respond to the needs of the underprivileged, the Master says, "Inasmuch as ye have done it unto one of the least of these my brethren, ye have done it unto me."

When we allow the spark of revenge in our souls to flame up in hate towards our enemies, Jesus teaches, "Love your enemies, bless them that curse you, do good to them that hate you, and pray for them which despitefully use you, and persecute you."

Everywhere and at all times, the love ethic of Jesus is a radiant light revealing the ugliness of our stale conformity....

Longfellow said, "In this world a man must either be anvil or hammer," meaning that he is either a moulder of society or is moulded by society. Who doubts that today most men are anvils and are shaped by the patterns of the majority? Or to change the figure, most people, and Christians in particular, are thermometers that record or register the temperature of majority opinion, not thermostats that transform and regulate the temperature of society....

Not a few men, who cherish lofty and noble ideals, hide them under a bushel for fear of being called different. Many sincere white people in the South privately oppose segregation and discrimination, but they are apprehensive lest they be publicly condemned. Millions of citizens are deeply disturbed that the military-industrial complex too often shapes national policy, but they do not want to be considered unpatriotic.... A legion of thoughtful persons recognizes that traditional capitalism must continually undergo change if our great national wealth is to be more equitably distributed, but they are afraid their criticisms will make them seem un-American. Numerous decent, wholesome young persons permit themselves to become involved in unwholesome pursuits which they do not personally condone or even enjoy, because they are ashamed to say no when the gang says yes....

SECTION II

Nowhere is the tragic tendency to conform more evident than in the church, an institution which has often served to crystallize, conserve, and even bless the patterns of majority opinion. The erstwhile sanction by the church of slavery, racial segregation, war, and economic exploitation is testimony to the fact that the church has hearkened more to the authority of the world than to the authority of God. Called to be the moral guardian of the community, the church at times has preserved that which is immoral and unethical. Called to combat social evils, it has remained silent behind stained-glass windows. Called to lead men on the highway of brotherhood and to summon them to rise above the narrow confines of race and class, it has enunciated and practiced racial exclusiveness.

We preachers have also been tempted by the enticing cult of conformity…. We have become showmen to please the whims and caprices of the people. We preach comforting sermons and avoid saying anything from our pulpit which might disturb the respectable views of the comfortable members of our congregations. Have we ministers of Jesus Christ sacrificed truth on the altar of self-interest and, like Pilate, yielded our convictions to the demands of the crowd?

We need to recapture the gospel glow of the early Christians, who were nonconformists in the truest sense of the word and refused to shape their witness according to the mundane patterns of the world. Willingly they sacrificed fame, fortune, and life itself in behalf of a cause they knew to be right. Quantitatively small, they were qualitatively giants. Their powerful gospel put an end to such barbaric evils as infanticide and bloody gladiatorial contests. Finally, they captured the Roman Empire for Jesus Christ.

Gradually, however, the church became so entrenched in wealth and prestige that it began to dilute the strong demands of the gospel and to conform to the ways of the world. And ever since, the church has been a weak and ineffectual trumpet making uncertain sounds. If the church of Jesus Christ is to regain once more its power, message, and authentic ring, it must conform only to the demands of the gospel….

SECTION III

Nonconformity in itself, however, may not necessarily be good and may at times possess neither transforming nor redemptive power. Paul in the latter half of the text offers a formula for constructive nonconformity: "Be ye transformed by the renewing of your mind." Nonconformity is creative when it is controlled and directed by a transformed life and is constructive when it embraces a new mental outlook. By opening our lives to God in Christ we become new creatures.... Only through an inner spiritual transformation do we gain the strength to fight vigorously the evils of the world in a humble and loving spirit....

This hour in history needs a dedicated circle of transformed nonconformists. Our planet teeters on the brink of atomic annihilation; dangerous passions of pride, hatred, and selfishness are enthroned in our lives; truth lies prostrate on the rugged hills of nameless calvaries; and men do reverence before false gods of nationalism and materialism. The saving of our world from pending doom will come, not through the complacent adjustment of the conforming majority, but through the creative maladjustment of a nonconforming minority.

Some years ago Professor Bixler reminded us of the danger of overstressing the well-adjusted life. Everybody passionately seeks to be well-adjusted. We must, of course, be well-adjusted if we are to avoid neurotic and schizophrenic personalities, but there are some things in our world to which men of goodwill must be maladjusted. I confess that I never intend to become adjusted to the evils of segregation and the crippling effects of discrimination, to the moral degeneracy of religious bigotry and the corroding effects of narrow sectarianism, to economic conditions that deprive men of work and food, and to the insanities of militarism and the self-defeating effects of physical violence.

Human salvation lies in the hands of the creatively maladjusted. We need today maladjusted men like Shadrach, Meshach, and Abednego, who, when ordered by King Nebuchadnezzar to bow before a golden image, said in unequivocal terms, "If it be so, our God whom we serve is able to deliver us.... But if not ... we will not serve thy gods"; like Thomas Jefferson, who in an age adjusted to slavery wrote, "We hold these truths to be self-evident, that all men are created equal, that they are endowed by their Creator with certain unalienable Rights, that among these are Life, Liberty and the pursuit of Happiness"; like Abraham Lincoln, who had the wisdom to discern that this nation could not survive half slave and half free; and supremely like our Lord, who, in the midst of the intricate and fascinating military machinery of the Roman Empire, reminded his disciples that "they that take the sword shall perish with the sword." Through such maladjustment an already decadent generation may be called to those things which make for peace.

Honesty impels me to admit that transformed nonconformity, which is always costly and never altogether comfortable, may mean walking through the valley of the shadow of suffering, losing a job, or having a six-year-old daughter ask, "Daddy, why do you have to go to jail so much?" But we are gravely mistaken to think that Christianity protects us from the pain and agony of mortal existence. Christianity has always insisted that the cross we bear precedes the crown we wear. To be a Christian, one must take up his cross, with all of its difficulties and agonizing and tragedy-packed content, and carry it until that very cross leaves its marks upon us and redeems us to that more excellent way which comes only through suffering....

We must make a choice. Will we continue to march to the drum-beat of conformity and respectability, or will we, listening to the beat of a more distant drum, move to its echoing sounds? Will we march only to the music of time, or will we, risking criticism and abuse, march to the soulsaving music of eternity? More than ever before we are today challenged by the words of yesterday, "Be not conformed to this world: but be ye transformed by the renewing of your mind."

Reprinted from *Strength to Love* by Martin Luther King, Jr.

Questions

1. In the letter to the Romans, Paul is concerned with understandings of faith that keep Jews and Gentiles in opposition to each other in the church. King understands this passage as calling Christians to not conform themselves to situations of injustice and racism. What in your situation does your faith call you to avoid or oppose?

2. Who are the people you admire who have been genuine non-conformists?

3. Would you describe your church as one that conforms, transforms, or both? How?

TWO

The Story of the Bible — A Drama in Ten Acts

At the Bible's heart is a story. That story begins with creation and ends with God's new creation. In between the story tells how God acts in history through a particular people, first Israel and then the church. The primary character in this story is God. It is by learning the story of the Bible that we learn about the God of the Bible.

There are many other types of literature besides narrative in the Bible. But to understand the background and message of most of the other types of literature it is essential to be able to place them in this basic narrative structure of the Bible. For example, the Ten Commandments in the book of Exodus begin with this statement: "I am the Lord your God, who brought you out of the land of Egypt, out of the house of slavery; you shall have no other gods before me." It is because God saved Israel from slavery that Israel is expected to respond by obeying the laws of the covenant. The narrative comes first; the commandments are a response.

But the biblical story as a whole is made up of many smaller parts that are often not clearly related to each other. Also, the narrative portions of the Bible are often interspersed with other types of literature. As a result it is extremely hard to get a sense of the whole sweep of the narrative. What follows is a brief overview of the Bible arranged in ten acts or segments. By getting a sense of the story as a whole, the individual stories and episodes and the way in which they refer to other aspects of the story will be clearer. For future reference, the biblical passages that contain the stories are included in the brackets at the beginning of each section.

ACT ONE: Stories of Creation and Corruption (Genesis 1–11)

In the beginning God created. The story of creation is told in two ways in the first chapters of Genesis:

- In the first chapter, God created the world and its inhabitants over a period of six days, culminating with the creation of humans, male and female. God then surveyed the whole creation and declared it very good and rested on the seventh day.

- The second chapter begins a longer account of the creation of the first human and how all the animals are brought to the human to be named. Because no suitable companion is found for the human, a second human is made from the first, and this is the beginning of sexuality, of male and female. These two are entrusted with a garden, with only one rule they must observe on pain of death. When they violate that rule, they are cast out from the garden and cursed with the suffering and struggle that are the human lot. The story of their children is the story of that curse working itself out.

Many generations later, God is disgusted with what humans have become and decides to wipe out the human race by a flood and begin again with only one family of righteous people, the family of Noah, who build a great ship (or ark) onto which they take specimens of every living creature. But after the flood, God is sorry for this destruction and makes a promise to the whole creation never again to destroy the earth. The rainbow is the sign of that promise.

The rest of the Bible is the story of God's efforts to save the creation from its curse through a specific people.

ACT TWO: The Ancestors of the Hebrews (Genesis 12–50)

God calls an elderly childless couple to leave their homes, promises them a blessing of land and descendants, and gives them new names, Abraham and Sarah. They make their way to this promised land called Canaan, the land that is now called Palestine or Israel.

Eventually Abraham and Sarah have a child, Isaac, who marries Rebecca.

They in turn have twins, Esau and Jacob, who are rivals for the inherited blessing of their father. Jacob is able to cheat his brother out of the blessing, and is given the new name Israel. He has twelve children by two wives, Leah and Rachel. These twelve children become the ancestors of the twelve tribes of Israel. Esau becomes the ancestor of Israel's neighbour and enemy, Edom.

One of Israel's sons, Joseph, is hated by his brothers, and they sell him into slavery in Egypt, where after many adventures, he becomes prime minister of Egypt because of his ability to interpret dreams. When, during a famine, his brothers come to Egypt to buy grain, he is reconciled with his family, and they stay on in Egypt.

ACT THREE: The Exodus (Exodus 1–20, 32–34, 40; Numbers 10–14)

Over the next four hundred years, the descendants of Israel become slaves in Egypt and come to be known as the "Hebrews."

But God hears their suffering, and raises up a leader named Moses, who hears God speaking from a burning bush and learns God's name, Yahweh or Jehovah, which means "I Am."

Then Moses confronts the Pharaoh of Egypt and demands that he let the Hebrews go. When the Pharaoh refuses, a series of plagues comes upon the people of Egypt. The tenth plague is the death of all the firstborn of Egypt, from the eldest son of the Pharaoh to the firstborn of their livestock. The Hebrews are spared from this plague by observing a sacrifice that is celebrated to this day as the Passover, because God passed over the Hebrews and did not kill their firstborn children.

The Hebrews are then allowed to leave Egypt, but later the Pharaoh changes his mind and sends an army into the desert after them. The Hebrews are saved again after they cross over a dry seabed, but the waters return and swallow up the pursuing Egyptian army when it tries the same crossing.

At Mount Sinai (also called Mount Horeb) the Hebrews make a covenant with God, and receive the Ten Commandments and many other laws from God as guidance in how to live in a way that pleases the God who saved them.

The Hebrews spend forty years in the wilderness of the Sinai, guided by a pillar of fire and smoke and sustained by "manna," bread that appears miraculously each morning.

Before the Hebrews enter the promised land, Moses dies. His farewell speech is depicted in the book of Deuteronomy.

ACT FOUR: The Conquest and Settlement of Canaan
(Joshua and Judges)

After Moses' death, the Hebrews are led by Joshua into the promised land of Canaan. Through a series of miraculous conquests, the Hebrews settle in the land.

They are organized loosely into a tribal confederacy, but are continually threatened by warlike neighbours. The real problem, however, is not their neighbours, but their failure to trust God and obey the law.

God raises up charismatic leaders called judges who inspire

the tribes to trust in God again and so they are able to defeat their enemies with God's help. These judges include Deborah, Gideon, Jephthah, and Samson.

ACT FIVE: Royal Scandals (1 and 2 Samuel, Ruth, 1 and 2 Kings, 1 and 2 Chronicles)

Facing the threat of a technologically superior enemy, the people of Israel decide that they need a king to unite and protect them. The prophet Samuel selects Saul as the first king, even though Samuel thinks having a king is a sign of lack of trust in God. Saul soon disobeys God, however, and is rejected as king.

Samuel chooses a shepherd named David to replace Saul as king, but Saul won't give up his throne so easily, so David spends years in hiding. Finally, Saul is killed in a battle with an army of Philistines, and David takes the throne about 1000 BCE. (I will be using the more inclusive terms BCE — before the common era — and CE — the common era — instead of BC and AD.)

David proves to be a great king, uniting the Hebrews and the remaining Canaanites into one nation, and choosing a former Canaanite city, Jerusalem, as his capital.

Although David is spectacularly successful as a general, greatly extending the borders of the nation, he is remembered also as a poet and the author of many psalms. As well, he is remembered as a very human king who seduces the beautiful Bathsheba and arranges for the death of her husband when she becomes pregnant. The prophet Nathan confronts David, who repents of his sin, but the child of this union dies.

After David's death, his son Solomon takes the throne and begins a series of ambitious building projects, including the great temple. Solomon is remembered as a wise king, but many of his policies divide the nation, and after his death the nation splits into a northern kingdom called Israel, and a southern one, called Judah.

The story of the monarchy from this point is the story of many bad kings who are confronted by faithful prophets like Elijah, Elisha, Amos, and Hosea.

Eventually the unfaithfulness of the kings of Israel leads to the defeat and destruction of Israel by Assyria in 721 BCE. Judah manages to survive, partly through the efforts of the prophet Isaiah, but the ten tribes of the northern kingdom are lost to history.

Judah is a small country caught between the great civilizations of Egypt and Mesopotamia. For the next century and a half, it struggles to survive with some dignity and autonomy. There are alliances, periods of brief independence and more alliances, but the most important theme is whether Judah will learn to trust in God. In addition to Isaiah, the prophets Micah, Zephaniah, Nahum, Habukkuk, and Jeremiah offer judgement and hope through this time.

ACT SIX: Exile (2 Kings 18–25)

In 596 BCE Judah meets its doom when it is conquered by the Babylonian Empire. Its mistaken hope that God would never allow Jerusalem to fall contributes to a suicidal rebellion in 587 BCE, and, as a result, many of its leading citizens are sent into exile in Babylon and the temple is destroyed.

The period of the exile is a period of intense questioning and transformation of the faith of Israel. The exile comes to be seen as the judgement of God on Israel for its lack of faithfulness to the law of God. Although it lasts somewhat less than fifty years, it is one of the most important periods in the history of Israel. During the exile, the prophets Jeremiah, Obadiah, Ezekiel, and Second Isaiah offered hope and guidance.

ACT SEVEN: Return and Rebuilding (Ezra, Nehemiah)

After the defeat of Babylon by Persia in 538 BCE the exiles are allowed to return to Israel.

Many of them stay in Babylon, but over many decades a trickle of exiles returns and tries to rebuild. The community remains poor and dispirited, however, until a group of exiles led by Ezra and Nehemiah begin in earnest the rebuilding of the temple and Jerusalem.

These two leaders also lead a renewal of commitment to the law of Israel, including an insistence on racial purity. It is probably in this period that many of the laws and writings that make up the Older Testament were collected and assembled.

INTERLUDE: The Period Between the Testaments

The period between the close of the Older Testament and the birth of Jesus is described in the book of Macabees, which is found in the Apocrypha and is not included in all Bibles (see chapter six).

Palestine is conquered by Alexander the Great, the famous

Macedonian general, in 332 BCE. When he dies his empire is split into three parts, one of which is the Seleucid Empire, ruled from Syria. Palestine becomes a part of this Empire.

One of the Seleucids, Antiochus IV Epiphanes, insists on being worshipped as a God. This is utterly unacceptable to the Jews, who worship only one God. They successfully rebel under the leadership of a family known as the Macabees, and live independently until they are conquered by the Roman Empire in 63 BCE.

ACT EIGHT: The Life of Jesus (Matthew, Mark, Luke, and John)

There are actually four different stories of Jesus' life in the four gospels, so this account will focus on what is common to them.

Two of the gospels begin the story with Jesus' miraculous birth in Bethlehem to a virgin named Mary. The other two begin the story of his life with the beginning of his public ministry and his baptism by John in the river Jordan, followed by the forty days he spends fasting in the desert near the Dead Sea.

He then travels through Galilee, Samaria, and Judea teaching about the Kingdom of God (or Kingdom of Heaven) and providing signs that God's reign is at hand: reaching out to outcasts, breaking down social barriers, healing, and performing miracles. He gathers a group of disciples, both male and female, from many walks of life, and chooses a core group of twelve.

There are signs that Jesus' ministry is threatening to some of the more powerful people in Palestine, who try to trap him into saying or doing something that will sabotage his ministry.

Many people begin to think of Jesus as the Messiah, but Jesus avoids accepting this title because many people thought of the Messiah as a military leader who would lead a rebellion against Rome. He teaches instead that he will suffer and die and be raised again.

Just before the festival of Passover, he goes to Jerusalem, entering the city on a donkey, an animal of peace, while his disciples wave palm branches. He spends time teaching in the temple, but stirs up antagonism when in righteous anger he drives merchants out of a section of the temple.

One night, Jesus eats a meal with his disciples, and tells them to remember him when they celebrate that meal. That night, one of his disciples betrays him and he is arrested, taken before a council of Jewish leaders, then before the Roman governor, and condemned and executed by being nailed to a cross. His body is hurriedly placed in a tomb because the Sabbath is about to begin, and no work can be done on the Sabbath.

After the Sabbath is over, women go to the tomb, but find it empty. The risen Jesus appears to several women and then to the other disciples.

ACT NINE: The Extension of God's Kingdom
(Acts, New Testament letters)

Fifty days after the resurrection of Jesus, the disciples experience the gift of the Holy Spirit during the festival of Pentecost in Jerusalem, and begin preaching the good news of Jesus to people from all over the world. This inaugurates the mission of the church.

The earliest Christians begin to teach and heal with the same power that Jesus displayed, believing that they are pioneers of the reign of God that had begun with Jesus. They continue the communal life taught them by Jesus, holding all their goods in common, and sharing it with all who were in need.

The church experiences antagonism and one of their leaders is stoned to death. The rest of the disciples have to flee throughout the country, but they use this opportunity to establish Christian communities in other cities.

A Pharisee named Saul is involved in this persecution, but an appearance of the risen Christ calls him to become the apostle to the Gentiles. He is renamed Paul and begins a series of missionary journeys to establish churches throughout the Roman Empire.

Up until this time all Christians have also been Jewish, but the church struggles with how to include Gentiles, and finally agrees that Gentiles do not have to become Jews in order to become Christians.

On one trip back to Jerusalem, Paul is arrested, but because he is a Roman citizen, he is sent to Rome to be tried by the emperor. Even in prison in Rome, Paul uses his time to spread the gospel.

At this point the story seems to break off without coming to a clear ending point. The story of the church does not end, but continues. The Bible is an open-ended story without a clear ending, because the resurrection means that the story of Jesus and the church continues in the lives of disciples from the first century to the present. The story of the Bible therefore includes us, and the narrative that begins in Genesis will continue through us to our descendants.

ACT TEN: The New Creation (Revelation, and parts of many books)

While the story of the Bible does not have a clear ending point, it does anticipate an ending that is itself a new beginning.

Although the earliest Christians believed that the kingdom of God had begun in the ministry of Jesus and the work of the church, they also believed that the kingdom will come in fullness only with a last judgement in which God will judge the whole world, purifying it of evil.

This judgement will inaugurate an eternal reign of peace and justice in which God will dwell intimately with God's people and the curse placed on creation will be overcome.

Exercises

1. To get a more in-depth overview of the story of the Bible than is possible here, read a children's story Bible from cover to cover. A children's story Bible is a selection of stories from the Bible retold in a way that makes them easier for children to understand. Be aware, however, that a children's Bible is not the same as the Bible itself. Since not everything can be included, the selection of what is included and is not included will depend on the author's understanding of what is important. In addition, the way a story is retold will depend on the author's beliefs about what a story means. There is nothing wrong with selecting and retelling, since it cannot be avoided. But it is important to be aware of the difference between a personal interpretation and the Bible itself.

2. Eventually you will need to read directly the major narrative sections of the Bible mentioned in the account above. Use the passages listed at the beginning of each Act in this chapter as a guide, and read one or two chapters at a time on a regular basis, perhaps before you go to bed at night, or as soon as you get up in the morning, or at a regular time during the day when you will not be interrupted. Many people use this type of pattern throughout their lives. Like all new habits, it will take some getting used to. If you miss a day or two, don't be discouraged; just get started again.

If you read a chapter a day, every day, you will be finished the narrative sections in 367 days. Two chapters a day would halve that time. You don't need to read this material in order. Try reading Genesis first and then Mark; when you have finished Mark, read Exodus and Numbers and then read Matthew. Give yourself a little variety. While you are doing this reading, start working on some of the other ingredients.

At the beginning, expect to find some of the material confusing. You will find some of the stories repeated, some of the details won't match. Sometimes you will find that it is difficult to figure out what happened. You may have strong emotional reactions to some of the stories. It may help to keep a journal or diary of your questions, thoughts, and ideas as you do this reading. Or make notes in the margins of your Bible. But don't let your questions and ideas bog you down. You will have the rest of your life to go back and work through the parts in more detail. You might also read it through like a novel so that you have a sense of the flow of the whole.

In doing this for the first time, many people encounter some surprises. One of the most common reactions is shock at the violence of much of the Bible. The vision of a warlike God in Joshua and Judges is totally at odds with the story of Jesus who taught us to love our enemies. This is only one of many tensions and contradictions that closer study will reveal. It is important to understand from the start that the Bible is not a book of easy answers. Those who assembled it had a taste for complexity and paradox. In that respect, the Bible is a mirror of life itself. That can be a challenge but don't give up! This is the second of the ingredients. As we add the rest it will become easier.

Review

In order to check and develop your knowledge of the biblical story, number the following events in the order in which they happen in the biblical narrative. To correct your answers see the key at the end of the chapter.

12   A   The prophet Elijah opposes corruption and false worship

19   B   Jesus drives money changers from the temple

5   C   Joseph becomes prime minister of Egypt

2   D   Noah builds the ark

11   E   The kingdom splits into northern and southern kingdoms

8   F   Israel is led by judges

20   G   The Holy Spirit inspires the early church at Pentecost

1   H   God creates the world

9   I   Samuel anoints David as king of Israel

22   J   A new heaven and a new earth are established

10   K   Solomon builds the temple

14   L   The prophet Jeremiah preaches in Jerusalem

21   M   Paul takes his missionary journeys

3   N   God calls Abraham and Sarah to leave their homeland

13   O   Israel is defeated by Assyria

16   P   Ezra and Neremiah encourage a new devotion to God's law

7   Q   Joshua leads the conquest of Canaan

17   R   Jesus is born in Bethlehem

6   S   Moses leads Israel through the desert

18   T   The sermon on the mount is preached

4   U   Jacob tricks Isaac to get his blessing

15   V   Judah is defeated and the Babylonian exile begins

KEY: A - 12, B - 19, C - 5, D - 2, E - 11, F - 8, G - 20, H - 1, I - 9, J - 22, K - 10, L - 14, M - 21, N - 3, O - 13, P - 16, Q - 7, R - 17, S - 6, T - 18, U - 4, V - 15

Another way in which people have interpreted the Bible is through storytelling. The story of the Bible and people's own stories are brought together in such a way that each informs the other. A good example of this is the retelling of Mark 5:25–29 by Elizabeth Amoah. A Methodist from Ghana, Amoah is lecturer in the Department for the Study of Religions at the University of Ghana in Legon.

The Woman Who Decided to Break the Rules

Elizabeth Amoah

> *And there was a woman who had had a flow of blood for twelve years, and who had suffered much under many physicians, and had spent all that she had, and was not better but rather grew worse. She had heard the reports about Jesus, and came up behind him in the crowd and touched his garment. For she said: "If I touch even his garments, I shall be made well." And immediately, the hemorrhage ceased; and she felt in her body that she was healed of her disease.*
>
> (Mark 5:25–29)

Naturally the weak, pale woman in this story was poor and frustrated. Added to her physical misery were the requirements of the Israelite ceremonial laws about impurities, as stipulated in Leviticus 15:19ff.

The plight of this woman would have been even worse had she lived in my country. Among the Akan of Ghana, women used to be considered abnormal during their menstrual period.

The custom was that, during the days of her period, a woman not only had to observe numerous restrictions — she was not allowed to cross the threshold of any man's house, nor was she allowed to perform the regular duties of a wife, like cooking the meals — but she even had to leave her own home and live alone in the *bra dan,* the "house for menstruation" on the outskirts of the village.

Hence, one of the euphemisms which the Akan used to describe a woman in her menstrual period was "she has gone to the outskirts of town," *w'ako mfikyire.*

The blood of such women was considered potent enough to neutralize or defeat evil powers. Parallel ideas are found in many other cultures.

Because of her disease, the unnamed woman with the hemorrhage whom Mark portrays must have suffered from financial problems. She also faced social, cultural, and religious difficulties. She had to move carefully, in order not to make someone else unclean by coming into contact with him or her.

The unnamed woman in this account had been living in that kind of frustrating isolation for twelve years. She had no hope of being healed — until Jesus came.

On the basis of the rules and regulations set forth in Leviticus 15, the woman must be very much aware that she ought not to go out and mingle with the crowd following Jesus.

Yet — whether out of superstition or out of a more genuine sort of trust and faith in Jesus — she is stubbornly convinced that if only she can touch even Jesus' garment all her years of frustration will be over.

Like any other person who has been hemmed in for years by traditions and customs she debates with herself. Should she try to touch Jesus and perhaps be healed? Or should she abide by the religious rules and live with her disease and frustration?

Whatever any of us might suppose to be the appropriate decision in similar circumstances, there is a proverb in Akan that is very much to the point: "It is the person who is very near the fire who feels how hot the fire is" [*nya oben gya no na onyim ma ogya no hyehye fa*].

This woman has been very near the fire. She knows what she has been going through for twelve long years. She knows how desperately she needs to be cured.

And so she decides to break the rules. She touches Jesus. That challenging and daring action results not only in her immediate healing but also in words of commendation from Jesus: "Daughter, your faith has made you well; go in peace, and be healed of your disease" (Mark 5:34).

In one sense the story of the encounter between the unnamed woman with a hemorrhage and Jesus is a woman's story. The presence of Jesus, it tells us, enables us to challenge and question all sorts of customs and traditions that enslave us and make us frustrated.

But the experience of this woman and the lessons this story teaches us represent a challenge to all Christians. They apply to all kinds of situations in human life.

True salvation always challenges existing laws and regulations. But it calls for awareness and effort on the part of the person who seeks salvation.

Reprinted from *New eyes for reading: Biblical and theological reflections by women from the third world,* edited by John S. Pobee and Barbel von Wartenberg-Potter.

Questions

1. Amoah draws on the customs of the Akan people for insight into the miracle story. Can making those connections be misleading? How does Amoah avoid that danger?

2. Amoah says "True salvation always challenges existing laws and regulations." Aren't some laws and regulations good? If so, how do we tell the good from the bad?

3. What are the customs and traditions in your situation that need to be upheld? Which ones need to be challenged?

A Tool Kit for Bible Study

THREE

If you were to take a course in carpentry, or auto mechanics, or cooking, one of the first things you would learn would be what tools or equipment would make your job easier, more accurate, and more consistent. There are similar tools for using the Bible. In this chapter you will learn how to use each of these tools so that the Bible can fully enrich your discipleship. All of these tools are written references that people use to help read the Bible. You won't use each of them every time you open the Bible, but knowing what they are means that you can turn to them when you need them. Some of these you may want to get for yourself, but many of them are reference books you could borrow from time to time. Every church library should have most of these resources, but some don't. If yours doesn't, ask why not, and check with your minister or a local library to see if you can borrow them there.

Translations

The most important tool is simply the Bible itself, which we always read in translation. The books that now make up the Bible were written originally in one of three ancient languages. Almost all of the Older Testament was written in Hebrew. Parts of the book of Daniel were written in Aramaic. All of the Newer Testament was written in *koine* Greek. Koine refers to a kind of Greek that was written by common people in contrast to the classical Greek of the philosophers and poets.

Therefore, unless you can read Hebrew and Greek you will be reading from a translation, and it is important to understand how the art of translation affects what we read. Language is embedded in culture, and there are many things in a language that simply cannot be translated into another language. The Inuit of Northern Canada, for example, have many different words for "snow." Snow is so much a part of their lives that they need to be able to distinguish the hard-packed snow that can be used for igloos from the soft, fluffy stuff that is useless for such a purpose. But in English we have only a few words for snow, and so in translation from

A sample of Greek text from the beginning of the Gospel According to Luke[1]

Inuktitut to English, some of the meaning is lost. Translating the Bible requires an attempt to render into a modern language not just the words, but the concepts of an entirely different culture. Try to imagine translating stories about shepherds and sheep into the language of a people (like the Inuit) who had never seen sheep and knew nothing about herding any kind of animal.

Bible translation is complicated by the fact that the Bible was assembled by members of ancient cultures. No one who is living today is a native speaker of those languages. That means that attempting to understand their language is always a process of reconstruction from historical sources. In addition, the Hebrew of the ancient poems and songs is not the same Hebrew as the relatively recent book of Ezra. Just as modern English has developed over several centuries, so has Hebrew. There is more difference between the Hebrew of various eras than there is between the English of today and that of Shakespeare's time! Shakespeare lived only 400 years ago, but the Bible contains language from a period covering *one thousand years*!

Finally, we do not have the original manuscripts of the Bible. We have copies of copies of copies. Because all of these copies were made by hand and mistakes are inevitable in a copy, there are differences among them. Any translation must assess the importance of these differences and decide which is closest to the original. Often a discrepancy will appear in only a small number of the many different early manuscripts that survive. Then it is relatively easy to decide which is the more ancient reading. But sometimes a difference will appear in many manuscripts. Then, scholars must make judgements about which of these manuscripts are the most reliable, and about how the differences might have come about. There are careful processes that have been developed over the years for making these decisions. Some of the most difficult choices are indicated in footnotes at the bottom of each page. Sometimes these notes will include references to ancient manuscripts that are translations into other languages like Greek or Syriac. Such notes indicate that the scholars had to make a difficult decision about whether an early translation was more genuine than a later Hebrew manuscript. More information about what these annotations mean can be found in the introductory articles at the beginning of the Bible you are using.

In summary, translations of the Bible can differ from each other because the translators made choices about which manuscript is the most accurate, because they do not agree about the meaning of a Hebrew or Greek word or phrase, or because they try different English ways of expressing something that is hard to translate. Given all of these problems, what is amazing is not that the versions differ from each other, but that they agree about as much as they do.

You might find this discussion of the complexities of translation intimidating, but it is not necessary to consider all of these issues every time you open your Bible. While the average reader depends on the expertise of scholars to produce accurate and scholarly translations, that does not mean that we do not need to be informed about what the scholars do.

A sample of Hebrew text from the book of Isaiah. Hebrew is written from right to left.[2]

One simple way to get informed is to compare translations. On the next page you will see three different translations of Luke 1:46–55 arranged in parallel columns. Read through them carefully and note the differences. Circle or highlight the differences that you think affect the meaning of the passage in a significant way.

The *New Revised Standard Version* attempts to reproduce as closely as possible the style of the original language. The *King James Version*, *Revised Standard*, *New International Version*, and *New American Bible* are other examples of this type of translation. The *Contemporary English Version* attempts to give an accurate translation in language that sounds more natural to English speakers. The *Today's English Version* (*Good News Bible*), *New English Bible*, the *Jerusalem* and *New Jerusalem Bible* are other examples of translations that follow this strategy. The *Cotton Patch Version* was written by Clarence Jordan, a biblical scholar and social activist from the southern United States, who tried to translate parts of the Bible in ways that made clear their implications for the racial tensions between whites and blacks. He attempts to translate not just the words but the ideas into language that Americans from the deep South would instantly understand. In that he comes close to a paraphrase. A paraphrase is different from a translation in that it tries to rewrite the Bible to make its language simpler or its meaning clearer for a particular group. Paraphrases usually interpret more and preserve less of the complexities and ambiguities of the original text. Paraphrases are usually done by individuals, while translations are prepared by

Luke 1:46–55

New Revised Standard Version

And Mary said,
"My soul magnifies the Lord,

and my spirit rejoices
    in God my Saviour,
for he has looked with favour on
    the lowliness of his
    servant.

Surely, from now on all
    generations will call me blessed;
for the Mighty One has done great
    things for me,
and holy is his name.

His mercy is for those who fear
    him from generation to
    generation.

He has shown strength with his
    arm;

he has scattered the proud in the
    thoughts of their hearts.
He has brought down the
    powerful from their thrones,

and lifted up the lowly;

he has filled the hungry with good
    things,
and sent the rich away empty.

He has helped his servant
    Israel,
in remembrance of his mercy,
according to the promise he made
    to our ancestors,
to Abraham and to his
    descendants forever."

Contemporary English Version

Mary said,
"With all my heart
    I praise the Lord;

and I am glad
    because of God my Saviour.
God cares for me,
    his humble servant.

From now on,
    all people will say
    God has blessed me.
God All-Powerful
    has done great things for me,
    and his name is holy.

He always shows mercy
    to everyone who worships him.

The Lord has used his
    powerful arm

to scatter those who are proud.
God drags strong rulers from their
    thrones

and puts humble people in
    places of power.

God gives the hungry good things
    to eat,
and sends the rich away with
    nothing.

God helps his servant Israel
and is always merciful to his
    people.
The Lord made this promise to our
    ancestors,
to Abraham and his family forever!

Cotton Patch Version

And Mary said,
"My soul exalts the Lord

And my heart exults
    before God my Savior.
For he has disregarded my
    humble origin,

And from now on the ages will
    honor me.
Great things the Almighty did for
    me,
And Holy be his name.

From generation to generation
His mercy showers those who fear
    him.

With his strong arm

And gives dignity to the lowly.

He loads the hungry with good
    things
But the rich he lets go with nothing
    at all.

Mindful of mercy, he gives a lift to
    his people
Just as he promised our
    fathers —
Abraham our father and his many
    descendants.

committees of scholars. J. B. Phillip's *Letters to Young Churches* and *The Living Bible* are other paraphrases.

It is important that you know what kind of Bible you are reading. Most Bibles contain introductions that explain the process used. If you use a paraphrase often, compare it frequently to a more literal translation to see how the paraphrase is interpreting the original. If you are buying a Bible, make sure you have an accurate translation and use a paraphrase as a secondary reference, if it is helpful.

One final note about the actual text we read: the biblical text is divided into chapters and verses. They were not a part of the original text but were developed long after. But because they are standard across all versions of the Bible in all languages, they make it easy for people to talk together about specific passages with greater ease and clarity. A number before the name of the book means there are two books with the same name. This may mean that there was originally one book that was split into two because only so much text could be put on one scroll (as was the case with the books of Samuel, Kings, and Chronicles), or because there were two or more letters written to the same church or attributed to the same author (1 and 2 Corinthians, 1 and 2 Thessalonians, 1 and 2 Timothy, and 1, 2, and 3 John). After the name of the book, the number before the colon refers to the chapter and the number after refers to the verse. For example the passage below is from the First Letter of Paul to the Church in Corinth, chapter 12, verses 12 and 13. That is usually abbreviated: 1 Corinthians 12:12–13 or 1 Corinthians 12^{12-13}.

> 12^{12} *For just as the body is one and has many members, and all the members of the body, through many, are one body, so it is with Christ.*^{13} *For in the one Spirit we were all baptized into one body — Jews or Greeks, slaves or free — and we were all made to drink of one Spirit.*

Other Resources

Study Bible

A study Bible includes the full text of a particular version of the Bible, together with some introductory articles, notes on the text, maps, and sometimes a concordance, a chronological table, a glossary, and other resources. Some study Bibles include more than one translation, arranged in parallel columns so they can be compared. If you are thinking of buying a Bible for yourself or a friend, a study Bible is a worthwhile investment.

Bible Atlas

The Bible is the story of a people and its relationship with the land. A Bible atlas is a useful way of learning about the land of the Bible and its history. Atlases are good for looking up particular places and often provide important clues for understanding a passage. The maps locate cities and show where borders were at particular periods of history. Most atlases also include articles and pictures that provide information about geography, climate, and archaeological discoveries that throw light on the Bible. Many ministers and church and public libraries will have a Bible atlas in their collections, but the maps in a good study Bible should be sufficient for most people most of the time.

Concordance

Many words have a richness of meaning that only becomes clear when you see how they are used in a variety of contexts. One way of understanding the meaning of a word in a particular passage is to find out how it is used in other passages. A concordance is a list of texts in which particular words or names appear.

Dictionary

A Bible dictionary is like a specialized encyclopedia, with short articles about words, people, places, books, and scholarly issues. Dictionaries can be found in one-volume or multi-volume form. For most students, one of the good one-volume dictionaries will be a useful resource.

Introduction

An introduction provides useful information that can assist in understanding the Bible. Introductions provide some of the information that scholars have discovered in their reading of these books. Many study Bibles have short articles that introduce each book. Longer articles may introduce groupings of books, or a particular type of literature such as wisdom. Introductions to the Older or Newer Testament, or to the Bible as a whole can be found in article form or as separate books. If you have a study Bible then take the time to read these articles. Some students may want to borrow a book-length introduction from a minister or a library or buy one.

Commentary

People who have made a special study of a book will often write a commentary that explores the text verse by verse. Most commentaries will print the text of a passage followed by discussions of its development, the meaning of the words, translation issues, the historical context, and its contemporary meaning. Some commentaries include new translations of the text. Like introductions and dictionaries, commentaries vary widely in the audience for which they are written. Some commentaries were written primarily for other scholars and will be nearly incomprehensible to the beginning Bible student. Find one that is written for someone with your level of knowledge.

Study Programs

Study programs are attempts to introduce the Bible or a part of the Bible in a systematic way. They include many of the resources named here, along with questions and exercises for individuals to explore the text and its implications for modern discipleship. There are a few such programs for individuals, but most are designed for groups.

Human Resources

In each region there are people with special expertise in the Bible. In addition to ministers, who have extensive training in the Bible, there may be Bible study groups going on in your congregation. There may be lay leaders who are experienced in individual or group Bible study. At regional levels there are often consultants associated with bible study programs like Kerygma or Bethel. If you are located close to a theological college, you may be able to take a course or consult with a professor there.

Review

In order to check and further develop your understanding of the content of this chapter, match the letter from the correct description with the name of the resource below. Check your answers against the key at the end of this chapter.

___ Version   ___ Study Bible   ___ Bible Atlas
___ Concordance   ___ Dictionary   ___ Introduction
___ Commentary   ___ Study Programs

A. A list of texts in which particular words or names appear, designed to help readers understand the meaning of a particular word by seeing how it appears in different contexts. Also useful for locating specific passages.

B. Resources designed to introduce the whole Bible, an individual book, or a biblical theme in a systematic way for individual or group study. They usually include a process for exploring the biblical text and making connections to our discipleship.

C. A specialized encyclopedia, with short articles about words, people, places, books, and scholarly issues.

D. A book that includes the full text of a particular version of the Bible, together with some introductory articles, notes on the text, maps, and sometimes a concordance, a chronological table, a glossary, and other resources.

E. Articles or books designed to provide basic information about the Bible or individual books. Some bibles include these before each book to explain the historical background, content, and other issues that will help people to understand what they are reading.

F. A verse by verse or section by section exploration of the biblical text with discussions of its development, the meaning of the words, translation issues, the historical context, and its contemporary meaning. Available for the whole Bible or for individual books.

G. A book that includes maps, articles, and pictures that provide information about geography, climate, and archaeological discoveries that throw light on the Bible.

H. A translation of the Bible from the original Greek or Hebrew. These translations differ because the translators make different choices about which Greek or Hebrew text is the most accurate, about the meaning of a Hebrew or Greek word or phrase, or because they try different English ways of expressing a concept.

Exercise

In order to get hands-on experience in using these resources, spend a couple of hours in a church library or another place where you can find them. Read through the first thirteen verses of the Gospel According to Mark. Read the introduction to Mark and the notes on these verses in a study Bible. See if you can figure out where the passage that Mark quotes from Isaiah comes from. You will get a surprise! Look up these places on a map: Judea, Jerusalem, Jordan River, Nazareth, Galilee. See if there is an article on the climate of Palestine in an atlas or dictionary and find out why the wilderness is called a wilderness. Find out what you can about Galilee. That will help you to understand why so many of Jesus' stories were about farming! Then look up "wilderness" and "John the Baptist" in a concordance and a dictionary. See if you can figure out what John's clothing was intended to symbolize and what significance wilderness held for the Jewish people. Finally, find a commentary and read what it has to say about Mark 1:1–13.

	B - Study Programs	F - Commentary
E - Introduction	C - Dictionary	A - Concordance
G - Bible Atlas	D - Study Bible	H - Version Key:

THREE   A TOOL KIT FOR BIBLE STUDY   43

THREE

A third way in which the Bible is read and interpreted is in Bible study groups, where the insights and knowledge of several people are shared and lead to new insights into the meaning of a particular text. This transcript of such a discussion took place in a base community in Solentiname, Nicaragua, while that country was ruled by the dictator Somoza. Until recently, the hierarchy of the Roman Catholic Church in Latin America has had close ties with the wealthy and powerful elites. This led many of the poor people, and the priests, nuns, and monks who served them, to look for a different kind of church that would take the concerns of the poor seriously. This, in turn, led to the development of base communities in which there are participatory worship, active lay leadership, and an effort to relate the gospel of Jesus Christ to the economic and political realities in which people live.

The Salt of the Earth and the Light of the World

Ernesto Cardenal

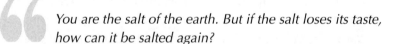

You are the salt of the earth. But if the salt loses its taste, how can it be salted again?

It is now no good for anything except to be thrown out and trampled by the people.

(Matthew 5:13)

ADAN: It seems to me it's because every meal should have salt. A meal without salt has no taste. We must give taste to the world.

JULIO: By liberating it. Because a world filled with injustice is tasteless. Mainly for the poor, life like that has no taste.

MARCELINO: You only need a little salt, because it's strong. You add just a tiny bit. There are only a few of us, but we can give taste to the world.

ONE OF THE ALTAMIRANOS WHO ARE FISHERMEN FROM DEER IS-LAND: Salt is also for preserving foods. A sawfish, a shad, we salt it and it keeps.

And DONA ADELA, a little old woman with a weak voice: We are the salt of the world because we have been placed in it so the world won't rot.

OSCAR, in a loud voice: But also we're a salt that sometimes doesn't salt for shit. That kind of Christianity we've got to get rid of because it does more harm than good.

OLIVIA: It seems to me that the salt has got lost when instead of preserving justice on earth, Christians have let injustice multiply more, as has happened now in capitalist society. We Christians wanted to prevent that, but we haven't. Instead, Christians have sided with injustice, with capitalism. We have sided with selfishness. We have been a useless salt.

FELIPE: Christianity that stopped being Christian, that's the salt that doesn't salt any more.

LAUREANO: Christianity that stopped being revolutionary, that lost its taste.

I (ERNESTO) said that once when I said Mass in Cuba, the gospel of that Sunday was this one about salt, and I told them in my sermon that the same thing had happened to their Christianity. It was salt that no longer salted and that's why it had been thrown out and trampled, because God wasn't interested in keeping a church like that.

ELVIS: It seems to me that the very same thing is happening right now here. Christians don't have that Christian taste. They're simple-minded, insipid. Only the ones who are struggling for a just society are the ones who have that taste of salt.

OSCAR: Ernesto, I'm going to ask you a question. Why is salt also considered to be a curse among us? When somebody has bad luck they say to him, "You're salted!"

I (ERNESTO) told Oscar that I didn't know. Perhaps it was because in ancient times when a conquering army wanted to lay waste a region it threw salt into the fields, the way the Americans now use defoliants. Jesus was probably not talking of salt in the sense of anything harmful but of something good. But salt and all the other things of the earth can be used for good or evil, as a blessing or a curse. I later said that in the gospel according to Saint Mark there is another sentence of Jesus about salt: "Have salt within you and live in peace one with the other." I asked if anybody wanted to comment on it.

PANCHO: I had always wracked my brains with that one, trying to understand it and not being able to. I was just going to ask you about it and now it's come up. I'm glad because I want to hear the explanation, what it means.

OLIVIA: It's like saying, "Love each other."

MARCELINO: I think that "salt" is the gospel word given to us so that we'll practice it and pass it on to others, practicing love, so that everybody will have it. Because salt is a thing that you never deny to anybody. When somebody is very stingy they say that "he wouldn't give you salt for a sour prune." That's why Jesus says "have salt," which means to have love shared out among everybody, and so we'll have everything shared out, we'll all be equal, and we'll live united and in peace.

PANCHO: Doesn't it probably mean that in spite of sin and injustice, which have always got to exist, and in spite of the salt or bad luck that is our lot, we must live in peace with one another, rich and poor?

LAUREANO answers quickly: How can we live in peace when some people are hurting others?

SILVIO (son of the leading merchant in San Carlos): Only with love can there be peace.

OLIVIA: It's all the same, "have love," "have salt."

MANUEL: Yes, because anyone who doesn't have salt is sick.

You are the light of the world. A city that is on a hilltop cannot be hidden.

(Matthew 5:14)

FELIX MAYORGA: Maybe the light is the *good* people, who practice love. Everyone that has a good spirit and loves others, he is the light of the world. They set the example and the people will follow them, as someone follows a person that carries a lamp to light up the darkness. Or let's suppose we're lost in the dark, and there's a light. The guy that's lost looks for the light.

MARCELINO: A lit up city that's on top of a hill can be seen from far away, as we can see the lights of San Miguelito from very far when we're rowing at night on the lake. A city is a great union of people, and as there are a lot of houses together we see a lot of light. And that's the way our community will be. It will be seen lighted from far away, if it is united by love, even though we don't have the city houses, just huts like the ones we have now, scattered here and there. But this union will shine and it's going to be seen from San Miguelito, from Papaturro, from San Carlos. And we may even get to be a city, too, because then we won't be in scattered huts the way we are now, and we'll have electric light, and when somebody goes by in a boat he'll see those lights of our union. But the thing that will shine most, and that's what Christ is talking about, is love.

Reprinted from *The Gospel in Solentiname*,
by Ernesto Cardenal, translated by Donald D. Walsh

Questions

1. Felipe said "Only the ones who are struggling for a just society are the ones who have that taste of salt." How is this similar or different to what Martin Luther King, Jr. was saying?

2. The interchange between Pancho, Laureano, and Silvio reflects some differences and disagreements about how the Bible should be understood. When can such differences and disagreements enrich our understanding of the Bible?

3. What do you think it would mean for you to be salt for the earth and light for the world in your situation?

It May Not Mean What You Think It Means!

FOUR

"A searing tale of passion, intrigue, and sin!" That could be the description on the back of any one of a thousand paperback novels published in the last decade. The word *sin* seems to sell books! Most people seem to think it refers to forbidden sexual pleasures. But in the Bible it has quite a different meaning. In the Bible, sin is not so much an act, but a state of being in separation from God. Paul's letters hardly ever use the term "sins" in the plural, for this reason. Paul is less interested in the actions, than in the state of alienation from God that gives rise to the actions.

Let me use an analogy. For a married couple, adultery is usually a sign of a deeper problem. The relationship has deteriorated to the point where partners are looking to satisfy their needs for intimacy in other relationships. To heal such a relationship, the couple must work through their deeper problems and re-establish the intimacy of their relationship. It is hard to forgive until that happens, but it is difficult for that to happen until the couple are ready to forgive. Sometimes a stalemate develops. According to Paul, our relationship with God is like that, but God took the first step towards a healing of our relationship, and helped to break through that alienation and reconcile us to God.

> *All this is from God who reconciled us to himself in Christ and has given us the ministry of reconciliation; that is, in Christ, God was reconciling the world to himself, not counting their trespasses against them and entrusting the message of reconciliation to us.*
>
> (2 Corinthians 5:18–19, *NRSV*)

> *It is [God] who, through Christ, bridged the gap between himself and us and who has given us the job of also bridging the gap. God was in Christ, hugging the world to himself. He no longer keeps track of [people's] sins, and has planted in us his concern for getting together.*
>
> (II Atlanta 5:18–19, *Cotton Patch Version*)

This state of alienation is also explored in the creation stories of Genesis, in which the roots of sin are described in a narrative of disobedience and the consequent loss of an intimate relationship with God. The garden of Eden is the description of what such an intimate relationship would be like. In Genesis 3 our alienation from God is symbolized by banishment from the garden. The word "sins" is also used in the Bible to refer to specific acts, but normally it assumes this more fundamental meaning of an act that is rooted in the deeper problem of a broken relationship. A "sin" is an act that destroys a relationship. In this sense a person can sin against God or against other people by doing things that break down the trust and capacity for a good relationship.

Justice is another word that is often misunderstood. For many people "justice" means "to get what you deserve." For them a justice system should punish people who do wrong and reward those who do right. But normally the Bible does not use "justice" in that way. It was one of the great insights of Martin Luther that the biblical concept of justice is one in which God seeks to reconcile broken relationships. For that reason, one of the ways in which God does justice is to forgive sins! But just forgiving sins does not restore a relationship if the person keeps doing things that break the relationship down. A person must be taught how to behave properly and sometimes convinced through punishment or reward that it is better to care for the relationship and not just for him- or herself. For that reason, the relationship between God and people is often described as that between a parent and a child, where the parent has the responsibility of lovingly correcting and instructing the child in constructive behaviour. God's judgement never means punishment or rejection, but is always corrective discipline that is intended to turn wayward children into co-operative friends.

In the same way that God's justice includes both judgement and mercy, in the Bible *just* or *righteous* people are not arrogant and judgemental, but generous and compassionate, and a just society is one in which the poor and vulnerable members are treated with generosity and compassion.

Sin and justice are only two of the hundreds of words in the Bible whose meanings must be understood in order to fully grasp the significance of passages. A list of some of the most important words with a brief indication of their biblical meaning and some important scripture references are given in the glossary at the end of this book.

Figures of Speech

The Bible is filled with word pictures or figures of speech. When speaking of such a mysterious reality as God, such figures of speech have the ability to open up understandings that could not be gained in any other way. These figures of speech are not just flowery decoration to make the language more attractive. In many fields of inquiry, from nuclear physics to poetry, metaphors and models are employed to gain understanding of things we have no other way of understanding. Think of electricity, for example. We use the metaphorical language of "current" "flowing" through a wire. This language is more literally used of water, but it serves very effectively to help us understand how electricity is available through wires. In fact we have no other way of speaking of electricity than through such metaphors.

The language the Bible uses to speak of God is very similar. The Bible often speaks of God as a person. This is metaphorical language; it speaks of a mysterious reality in language of something more familiar to us. This is often a problem for modern people who are used to thinking more concretely. Sometimes a guide to the most common images can help to clarify the concept.

Some of these common figures of speech, together with some of the key passages in which they are used and suggestions about their symbolic meaning are included in the glossary. You will discover many more as you work your way through the Bible. When you encounter a figure of speech, it is helpful to engage your creativity rather than just your intellect. Try free-association. In other words, what comes to mind for you when you think of "fire" or "rock" or "water"? You may find it helpful to write down some of these thoughts, draw a simple picture, or use some form of creative expression that is helpful for you. You can use the glossary in this book, a biblical dictionary, or a concordance to discover more about how these figures of speech are used in the Bible.

Review

Match the following words with the appropriate descriptions. Some of the descriptions apply to more than one of the words. Consult the glossary for words that you are unsure of. The key is located at the end of the chapter.

__	1. Angel	A	to overlook a person's sins in order to establish a right relationship
__	2. Apostle	B	"the anointed one" who was to establish God's reign of peace
__	3. Blood	C	the state of right relationships that God desires for and with the creation; a synonym for "peace" and the "kingdom of God"
__	4. Body of Christ		
__	5. Bread	D	translates the Hebrew word shalom and means the presence of right relationships among all God's creatures
__	6. Call		
__	7. Church	E	a symbol of death and destruction as well as the symbol of life and new birth
__	8. Covenant		
__	9. Disciple	F	a symbol of the Holy Spirit; the same word as "spirit" in both Hebrew and Greek
__	10. Faith		
__	11. Fear of God	G	Jesus taught about this relationship between God and God's creation in which God's will is done "on earth as in heaven"
__	12. Fire		
__	13. Gospel	H	God's generosity, which is not based on anything we do
__	14. Grace	I	a person sent forth with the message of Jesus Christ
__	15. Justify	J	a word that means "good news"
__	16. God's Kingdom	K	a symbol of the power and energy of God
__	17. Law	L	respect, reverence, and obedience to God
__	18. Light	M	a symbol for all food and for Jesus' body
__	19. Love	N	a student or follower
__	20. Messiah/Christ	O	includes both instruction about how to live and behaviour that is forbidden
__	21. Peace		
__	22. Repentance	P	a relationship made formal through promises and commitments
__	23. Salvation		
__	24. Sin	Q	the choice to do good to someone else
__	25. Water	R	God's invitation to co-operate in God's action
__	26. Wind	S	to turn around and change the way we live
		T	symbolizes the church
		U	a state of alienation from God, OR an act that is destructive of relationship
		V	belief, trust, and obedience
		W	symbolizes the life of an animal or person
		X	a messenger from God
		Y	an assembly or congregation of people, usually refers to the band of Jesus' followers

Exercises

1. Skim through the glossary and choose three of the words listed there to explore further. Read the definitions, and look up the scripture readings listed. If possible, also look them up in a Bible dictionary. Note your own discoveries about each word in the space below or the margins of the glossary. Also, try to think of other words that mean the same thing, and others that mean the opposite. For example: one of the opposites of "sin" is "love," while synonyms might be "alienation," "broken-ness," and "division."

2. Another helpful exercise is to incorporate the learning of these words into a devotional practice. Take one word each day, read the definition in the glossary and look up the scripture refer-ences. Then try the imaginative exercises mentioned above.

Key: 1 - X, 2 - I, 3 - W, 4 - T, 5 - M, 6 - R, 7 - Y, 8 - P, 9 - N, 10 - V, 11 - L, 12 - K, 13 - J, 14 - H, 15 - A, 16 - G, 17 - O, 18 - K, 19 - Q, 20 - B, 21 - D, 22 - S, 23 - C, 24 - U, 25 - E, 26 - F

Two Reflections on Repentance

One of the ways in which the Bible is interpreted is through the church's liturgy. Liturgy refers to the prayers, music, and readings that are part of worship. These two short reflections give examples of the use of the Bible in the liturgy of the Orthodox churches of Eastern Europe and the Middle East. In the first reading, the word *Theotokos*, which means "God-bearer," refers to Mary the mother of Jesus. The passage from Luke on which the selection is based is often called the "Magnificat."

A Turning Point in Her Life

Dimitra Koukoura, Greece
(based on Luke 1:46–55)

Maria was a drug addict. After she was cured, she took part in a television round-table discussion on the growing drug problem. The programme presented statistical data, sociological explanations, police reports, legal perspectives, etc. Among all the learned presentations Maria's simple testimony stood out.

Maria said: "When I was first involved in drugs, my life had no meaning. My family gave me whatever I asked for. I was at the centre, and the world revolved round me. Indeed I was a poor, empty girl. I had no time for a flower or a bird; I had no concern for the poor or the victims of injustice. When I was undergoing treatment at a foundation, I longed to get back to the cocaine friends. Then, walking in the park one August evening, I heard the Magnificat being sung at the foundation chapel. That was the turning point of my life. Our Lady Theotokos spoke to me through her song. She invited me to commit myself to her son, our Lord, and find meaning and love in my life."

During the first 13 days of August, every evening there is a special service for Theotokos in our churches. Maria must have heard the Magnificat sung at one of these services. The experts on narcomania listened to her testimony with a certain ironic sympathy.

Reprinted from *Come Holy Spirit — Renew the Whole Creation:*
Six Bible Studies

A Prayer to the Holy Trinity

Qais Sadiq, Lebanon
(based on Mark 1: 4–13)

In the desert of our petrified souls, without shade or water, appears John the Baptist, calling upon us to repent, and to look upon the Lamb of God who carries our sins. Then the Lord appears, sanctified by the Father's Spirit and blessed by his voice. Let us worship the Holy Trinity for the salvation that Christ brings to us.

Holy Father, you called us out of the desert of our sins to share in your everlasting kingdom. Help us by the power of your Spirit to live in your presence.

Holy Son, you have by your humility blessed the waters of Jordan; bless our life, and send your Holy Spirit to abide with us and renew us from within.

Holy Spirit, purify our bodies, sanctify us, and make us a temple where you will be permanently present.

Holy Trinity, bless our coming together in your name. Deliver us from the evil one, lead us into your truth, and renew in us the image and likeness of your being, for you are both the source and goal of our life. Amen.

Reprinted from *Come Holy Spirit — Renew the Whole Creation: Six Bible Studies.*

Questions

1. Maria finds freedom and healing through committing herself to Jesus. Have you ever had an experience like Maria's? How does commitment lead to freedom?

2. In the "Prayer to the Holy Trinity," the desert in which John the Baptist preached is interpreted as "the desert of our petrified souls" and "the desert of our sins." What do you think of such an interpretation? Does it describe your own soul?

The Bible Is Not a Book! It Is a Library!

The Italian city of Verona, fictional home of Juliet in William Shakespeare's tragic romance *Romeo and Juliet*, receives thousands of letters a year addressed to Juliet. The vast majority of these letters are from desperate lovers seeking Juliet's advice. So Verona employs someone to answer those letters. Such an inability to understand that Shakespeare's play is a work of fiction may be a harmless foolishness for most of those who write such letters. For those who read the Bible, however, an inability to distinguish the types of literature it contains can lead to serious misunderstandings.

The word "Bible" comes from the Greek *biblia,* which means, simply, "little books." While it is normally found bound together between two covers for convenience, the Bible is actually a library of different kinds of literature.

Think of your local public library. If you go there you will find a reference section with encyclopedias, dictionaries, atlases, and the like. You will find a children's section crammed with picture books, fairy tales, and nursery rhymes. You will find a fiction section with novels and collections of short stories. You will find poetry, science texts, biographies, volumes of music, and a host of other kinds of writing. They are not all the same, and if you pick up an automotive repair manual expecting to read a detective story, you will be disappointed.

The Bible is the same. If you open a Bible to the table of contents, you will find sixty-six different titles,[1] ranging from erotic poetry (*Song of Songs*) to a short work of fiction with a moral theme (*Jonah*). In many of the books, different types of literature are found within the same book. In *Exodus*, for example, there are equally long stretches of narrative and legal material, with a few poems and songs thrown in. As you can imagine, it helps to know a little about what kind of literature you can expect to find.

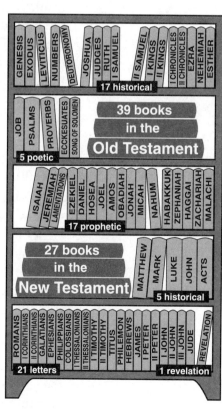

The following are some of the more important types of writing you will find in the Bible, along with some other examples of the same kind of literature.

Myth

The word "myth" is usually used to mean something that is commonly believed but is untrue. But it also has a deeper meaning. As we use it to refer to parts of the Bible, it means a story that speaks of ultimate or universal realities in terms of the everyday. The first eleven chapters of Genesis, for example, explore such issues as the nature of reality, human nature and destiny, and evil and suffering. They do this through deceptively down-to-earth stories of humans and a God who walks and talks like a human. Myths speak of profound truths in such down-to-earth ways. They shape the way we think about the world and what it means to be human. It makes a real difference, for example, whether we think of the world as having been created or as having occurred through chance. Or whether we think that the world is the way God wants it, or whether we think of it as "fallen." What myths do not do is give a scientific or historical explanation about how the world was made. To read them as science or history rather than myth is to profoundly misunderstand them and to miss the real point of what they teach. Other examples include creation and flood stories from other cultures and the stories of Greek and Roman gods. Some people would describe western movies or the Star Wars movies as myths, because of the way they depict life as a struggle between good and evil, sharply defined.

Legend

These stories are like myths, but tend to be less universal in their themes. Legends account for places (for example, the pillar of salt in Genesis 19), the names of places or people (e.g., Peniel and Israel in Genesis 32:22–32), and the practices or customs of a people. Other legends deal with the ancestors and heroes of a cultural group as a way of identifying that group and distinguishing it from others (e.g., the accounts of Isaac and Ishmael, Jacob and Esau, and the Judges and David). Legends have varying degrees of historical accuracy. They are told, however, not primarily for historical purposes, but to shape the identity of a people. Other examples include the stories about George Washington in the United States and King Arthur and Robin Hood in England.

Historical Narrative

Biblical history is never history for the sake of history. It is always an attempt to recall past events in order to point to their implications for how people might be faithful to God in the present. Events are chosen, shaped, and retold in order to make a point. This process can easily be seen in the way that the author of Chronicles retold the narratives from Kings. Because the author of Chronicles had a different point to make than the author of Kings, there are numerous places where the two narratives contradict each other. The process can also be seen in the book of Judges, which is organized around a recurring pattern: disobedience leads to danger which leads to repentance. In response God sends a saviour or judge, but when the danger is gone, the people slip back into disobedience, and the cycle repeats itself. The historical books of Judges, Samuel, Kings, Chronicles, Ezra, and Nehemiah in the Older Testament and Acts in the Newer Testament draw out different themes with their narratives, but they share a common approach to history. A modern example is the way that the events leading up to World War II have been interpreted as offering lessons for the present. The danger of Chamberlain's policy of appeasement is invoked by those who favour military preparedness. Those who emphasize common security (the idea that none of us is safe if justice and fairness are not enshrined in international relations) point to the impact of the deterioration of the German economy resulting from the heavy reparations imposed after World War I.

Legal Material

The laws of the Bible are concentrated almost entirely in its first five books. Many of these laws are similar to the laws of other societies in the ancient Near East in their conditional or "casuistic" character. These types of laws specify the penalty for particular acts, and detail the criteria that are to be taken into account for judgement. The kind of law found in the Ten Commandments is more specific to the Bible. In this form of law, behaviours are either commanded or prohibited. Individual laws of both types were collected into five main groups:

- the Decalogue or Ten Commandments (Exodus 20:2–17 and Deuteronomy 5:6–21)

- the Covenant Code (Exodus 20:22–23:33)

- the Priestly Code (Exodus 25:31; Exodus 34:29–Leviticus 16 and portions of Numbers)

- the Holiness Code (Leviticus 17–26)

- the Deuteronomic Code (Deuteronomy 12–26)

These codes show signs of being developed at different times by different people with different interests, but because Moses was seen as being the great lawgiver of Israel, they were all in one way or another attributed to him. In addition to the criminal and civil laws of a society, modern examples include the ethical codes of professional societies and corporations.

Psalms and Songs

Songs are some of the oldest material in the Bible. Many scholars, for example, believe that the song of Miriam in Exodus 15:21 is the oldest verse in the Bible. A variety of songs scattered throughout the Bible express joy, praise, sadness, guilt, pain, longing, and hope. But the largest concentration is found in the book of Psalms. Many of the Psalms were originally used in the temple. They are like a modern hymn book! Some of them were used on specific occasions, like the coronation of a king, or a time of national danger like a war or famine or plague. Others were used by individuals to express fear, confession, hope, or thanksgiving.

Wisdom

Wisdom is less a type of literature than it is a literary tradition that is focused on the theme of succeeding in life. It shares certain common themes but uses a variety of literary forms, ranging from short proverbs (see Proverbs) to complex discussions of the meaning of life (see Ecclesiastes), from a narrative that integrates wisdom themes into the account of Israel's origins (the story of Joseph in Genesis 37– 50) to a poetic exploration of suffering in relation to a just God (Job). There are many modern equivalents, ranging from common proverbs to self-help books, from novels to the most sophisticated philosophy.

Prophecy

It is sometimes believed that prophecy is predicting the future, but this is an over-simplification. Prophecy is an attempt to point out God's purposes and God's intentions and desires in a particular situation. The prophets do indeed sometimes point to future events, but these projections into the future are always warnings about what will happen if God's messages are ignored or promises about consequences if God is not taken seriously. It seems to have been common in ancient times for the king to consult or even employ prophets. King David's prophet Nathan (see 2 Samuel 7) is the best-known example. Other prophets arose and spoke without royal permission, but there seems to have been some tolerance for their activities. Prophets generally spoke in short poetic utterances called *oracles*. Some prophets, like Ezekiel also used symbolic acts to make their point more vivid. These utterances were probably collected and written down later by their disciples. Most of the prophetic books are collections of these oracles with little explanation of the historical background that prompted them. There is really no modern equivalent to the ancient prophets, but social activists who speak out about social evils and participate in symbolic acts of protest are close.

Apocalypse

Daniel, Revelation, and parts of other books (see especially Mark 13) focus specifically on visions of the end of the world and the glories of the age to come. These writings usually were written in times when a faith community was being persecuted. The book of Revelation was written during the period of persecution of Christians by the Roman Empire, while Daniel was written during the occupation of the Jewish nation by the Syrian Empire in the second century BCE. Apocalyptic literature includes bizarre images of angels, demons, dreams, trances, and a judgement in which the faithful will be vindicated and their persecutors will be punished. Because this type of writing is produced by small, persecuted groups, it is not understood or appreciated by the dominant society. So the closest modern equivalents would be found among racial or religious groups that are persecuted by the majority.

Parable

One of the primary ways in which Jesus taught his disciples was through parables. Jesus' parables usually make a comparison between the reign of God and a story or commonly known activity or object. Like a joke, the parable often leads up to a "punch line" that includes a surprise or shock making us think about things in a new way. For example, the parable of the Lost Sheep and Lost Coin in Luke 15:1–10 forces those who think about God as being primarily interested in the "godly" to consider that God's priorities might be different. The closest modern equivalents would be found in some kinds of short stories.

Miracle Stories

The stories of Jesus' miracles were shaped by being told and retold by Jesus' followers over a number of decades, before they were ever written down. This shaping created a standard format in which there was a setting, a cure, and a response from the crowd or the person cured. The miracle stories in the life of Jesus usually emphasize the importance to the cure of faith. See, for example, Mark 5:21–43, where two miracles are combined into one story. While they may be difficult for those raised in our modern scientific culture to appreciate, miracle stories were seen by ancient people as important signs of the power of God at work in Jesus and his followers.

Gospel

Matthew, Mark, Luke, and John, the four gospels that tell the stories of Jesus' life, death, and resurrection are not modern biographies. They tell little of Jesus' early life. Matthew, Mark, and Luke are attempts to retell the stories of the public ministry of Jesus in such a way as to make his significance clear for a new generation of followers. Like myth, legend, and historical narrative, therefore, the primary focus is not on historical accuracy, but on the meaning of what Jesus did and said. Each gospel writer selected, edited, and shaped the traditions and memories of Jesus in order to make these meanings clear. John is a different kind of gospel again, in which the primary focus is on who Jesus was. By crafting a series of dialogues between Jesus and inquirers, John places his own theology in the mouth of Jesus. We will explore the gospels in more detail in chapter six. The gospel is a unique form of literature that seems to have been invented by those who wrote them. I know of no modern equivalent.

Epistle

An epistle is an ancient letter. Modern letters usually begin with "Dear So and So" and end with "Yours Sincerely." Ancient letters had the name of both the writer and the recipient at the beginning. The first part of the letter was a thanksgiving for the person being written to after which the business of the letter began. After the main text was finished, greetings were extended to other people known by the writer who were in contact with the person addressed. The following is a letter that could easily have been written in the ancient world:

> Andreas to his father and mother, greetings.
>
> I hope all goes well with you. I'm constantly thinking of you. Unfortunately, I've had a great misfortune. Today I was kidnapped by robbers. They want half a talent of silver as ransom and give you thirty days to pay it in. They have threatened to kill me and the others. But be confident: I got out of the Roman prison, so I shall get out of this one too.
>
> Greetings to Baruch!
> Timon and Malchus will bring this letter.
> Peace be to you all.[2]

If you look carefully at many of the letters in the Newer Testament, especially the letters of Paul, you will find this arrangement. See, for example, the letter of Philemon, among the shortest letters. In our own time, it is fairly common for the letters of famous people to be collected and published. These letters shed light on both their personal lives and their thought and work.

Review

Choose the best answer that applies.

1. The "myths" in the Bible are:
   A. found in the early chapters of Genesis
   B. explain in scientific terms how the world was made
   C. stories which speak of profound truths in terms of the everyday
   D. all of the above
   E. A and C only

2. The historical books of the Bible:
   A. include the books of Joshua, Judges, Samuel, Kings, and Chronicles, among others
   B. retell events in order to teach what God did in the past
   C. use stories of the past to teach how people might be faithful to God in the present
   D. all of the above
   E. A and B only

3. Songs and Psalms:
   A. are all found in the book of Psalms
   B. some are among the oldest material in the Bible
   C. express a variety of emotions including joy, fear, sorrow, guilt, hope, and thanksgiving
   D. all of the above
   E. B and C only

4. The wisdom tradition includes which of the following:
   A. short proverbs
   B. ecclesiastes — a discussion of the meaning of life
   C. the story of Joseph (Genesis 37–50)
   D. Job — a poetic exploration of suffering in relation to a just God
   E. all of the above

5. Prophecy is best described as:
   A. the effort to predict the future
   B. the attempt to point out God's intentions and desires in a particular situation
   C. a tradition of people and writings about God's judgement and grace in history
   D. all of the above
   E. B and C only

6. A parable:
   A. is a short story about something fairly ordinary
   B. has a surprise ending like a joke
   C. is one of the ways Jesus taught about the reign of God
   D. is intended to change the reader by helping us think in a new way
   E. all of the above

7. Which of the following statements about "gospels" are true: They
   A. retell the stories of Jesus' life, death and resurrection
   B. were written primarily in order to teach what it means to follow Jesus
   C. each have a slightly different understanding of the significance of Jesus
   D. all of the above
   E. A and C only

8. Which of the following are true about "epistles": They
   A. are ancient letters
   B. usually have the names of both the sender and the recipient at the beginning
   C. were written to encourage and instruct early Christians
   D. all of the above
   E. A and C only

9. Which of the following are true about "apocalypses": They
   A. were usually written to encourage people being persecuted
   B. are found in both Older and Newer Testaments
   C. are written in highly symbolic language that is often difficult to decipher
   D. speak of God's triumph over evil and oppressive forces
   E. all of the above

Exercises

1. To test yourself, try opening your Bible randomly at several places and placing your finger on a passage. See if you can identify what type of literature you have located. If you can't, turn to the introduction to the book you are reading (if your Bible has them) and see if that helps.

2. Look up in a Bible dictionary the types of literature that still seem strange to you. Try to put the information you find into your own words.

Key: E is the right answer for all the questions except 2, 7, and 8, for which D is the right answer.

FIVE

READING

Two Hymns

One of the most important ways in which the Bible is interpreted is in the music of the church. Hymns and choral music provide significant reflections on the meaning of many biblical passages. These two hymns are reflections on the meaning of the Lord's Supper or Eucharist, as recounted in 1 Corinthians 11:23–26, Mark 14:22–25, Matthew 26:26–29, and Luke 22:15–20. The first is by Thomas Aquinas (1225–74), a Dominican monk who was one of the most important theologians in the history of the church. The second is by William Henry Turton (1856–1938), an English army engineer who wrote this hymn for a service celebrating the anniversary of an English church union.[3]

1. Now my tongue, the mystery telling,
   of the glorious body sing,
   and the blood, all price excelling,
   which the nation's Lord and King,
   once on earth among us dwelling,
   shed for this world's ransoming.

2. That last night, at supper lying
   with the twelve, his chosen band,
   Jesus with the law complying
   keeps the feast its rites demand;
   then, more precious food supplying,
   gives himself with his own hand.

3. Word made flesh, by word he maketh
   very bread his flesh to be;
   man in wine Christ's blood partaketh:
   and if senses fail to see,
   faith alone the true heart waketh
   to behold the mystery.

4. Therefore we, before him bending,
   this great sacrament revere;
   faith her aid to sight is lending;
   though unseen, the Lord is near;
   ancient types and shadows ending,
   Christ our paschal Lamb is here.

Translated by Edward Caswall (1814–78) and others.

1. Thou, who at thy first eucharist didst pray
   that all thy church might be for ever one,
   grant us at every eucharist to say
   with longing heart and soul, Thy will be done.
   O may we all one bread, one body be,
   through this blest sacrament of unity.

2. For all thy church, O Lord, we intercede;
   make thou our sad divisions soon to cease;
   draw us the nearer each to each we plead,
   by drawing all to thee, O Prince of peace;
   thus may we all one bread, one body be,
   through this is blest sacrament of unity.

3. We pray thee too for wanderers from thy fold;
   O bring them back, good Shepherd of the sheep,
   back to the faith which saints believed of old,
   back to the church which still that faith doth keep:
   soon may we all one bread, one body be,
   through this blest sacrament of unity.

4. So, Lord, at length when sacraments shall cease,
   may we be one with all thy church above,
   one with thy saints in one unbroken peace,
   one with they saints in one unbounded love:
   more blessed still, in peace and love to be
   one with the trinity in unity.

Questions

1. Aquinas speaks of the presence of Christ's body and blood in the bread and wine as a "mystery" that is to be revered. What reverence do you hold for the bread and wine of communion?

2. Turton refers to the Lord's Supper as "this blest sacrament of unity." What ethical implications can you see in the communion meal?

3. In what ways is the understanding of communion displayed in these two hymns similar to or different from that of your church? If you don't know, how could you find out?

How the Bible Came to Be

Students usually go through a number of stages in writing an essay. They start with a topic, do research, take notes, write an outline, and finally write the text of the essay itself. The final text may be written and rewritten many times. An immature or unscrupulous student might plagiarize some of the materials used for research. It is often easy for teachers to spot plagiarism, though, because the style of language is often quite different than what the student usually writes. An observant teacher can usually make some fairly accurate guesses about what kind of research a student did and what process was used to produce the essay.

We can do the same thing with the Bible, except that it is much more difficult, for the Bible went through a complex process of development over more than a thousand years.

A brief description of this process is described in the opening verses of the Gospel According to Luke 1:1–3.

> *Since many have undertaken to set down an orderly account of the events that have been fulfilled among us, just as they were handed on to us by those who from the beginning were eyewitnesses and servants of the word, I too decided, after investigating everything carefully from the very first, to write an orderly account for you, most excellent Theophilus.*

Luke mentions that others have written accounts of the life of Jesus, and that these accounts in turn were based on the memories and teachings handed on by the original disciples, who no longer seem to be available. Luke therefore provides evidence that there were at least two stages of his work, which I will call the oral tradition and the written tradition. The word *tradition* refers to the process of each generation passing on the elements of the tradition to the next generation. These two kinds of tradition can also be identified in much of the rest of the Bible. There is also a third stage that Luke doesn't mention because it happened after he finished writing his book. This third stage is the formation of the canon. The word *canon* means "ruler" or "measuring stick." A canon is formed when a collection of books is established as the ruler of a community's faith and practice. Other books are not usually prohibited, but community members are to measure everything against the ruler of the canon. The canon becomes the focus for what was considered to be faithful to the traditions of the community of faith.

For the moment I will describe each of these stages briefly and then illustrate how they influenced the development of the Pentateuch (the first five books of the Bible) and the gospels.

Oral Tradition

The societies that produced the Bible were all primarily oral cultures. That means that most of the people could not read, and most information was received through hearing, stored in people's memory and passed on by retelling. Much of the Bible originated as material that was passed on in this way, usually for many generations. In our time, riddles, jokes, and ghost stories are mainly part of an oral tradition. Grimm's Fairy Tales are good examples of material that originated and was passed on in oral form and was collected and written down later. Much biblical material also shows signs of this kind of origin. Songs and poetry, short stories, proverbs, and simple codes of laws like the Ten Commandments are the easiest things to remember and pass on. Stories tend to be pared down to their simplest and most important elements. This is why many of the stories in the Bible sound like a lot has been left out of them.

> WARNING The amount of detail in this chapter may make your head hurt! You do not need to memorize it all. Read for understanding, so that you know the basic steps involved.

Written Tradition

At certain points people collected the stories, songs, and laws that were part of the oral tradition and wrote them down. Usually the writer would adapt or add original written material to provide a context. A good example is in the book of Job. The remnants of a folk tale can be seen in the first two chapters and the last chapter. The author may have taken a folk tale circulating in oral form, written it down, replaced the middle with an extended poetic discussion of the problem of suffering and evil and then adapted the ending. The letters of Paul are mostly original written material but sometimes include sayings, teachings, or hymns that were part of the oral tradition at the time. See Philippians 2 for the use of an early Christian hymn.

Writers also used other written works as sources. For an example see the references to "The Book of the Acts of Solomon" in 1 Kings 11:41, "The Book of the Chronicles of the Kings of Israel" in 1 Kings 14:19, and "The Book of the Chronicles of the Kings of Judah" in 1 Kings 14:29. Those references are unusual, however. Most sources are not acknowledged in this way. There were no copyright laws or footnoting procedures then! Most sources can only be identified by careful reading, observing odd breaks and disjunctions in the material, and noticing differences or similarities in style, vocabulary, and theology. If you notice that a certain story is repeated, with differences in each version, that is a sign that different versions of the story were probably contained in two different sources that were included in the final text.

Just because something was written down did not mean that it could not be changed. In our age of printing presses and photocopiers it is easy to overlook how labour-intensive it was to copy a book. It was quite common for written materials to be altered or adapted in this copying process, either intentionally or by accident.

Often the writers of these books were anonymous, but sometimes, particularly in letters, the author is named. But sometimes the person who is named is not the person who wrote the book. There was an ancient practice in which an author would attribute the book or letter to a famous person of the past. This process was not a cynical attempt to deceive the readers or to get people to read a work. It was a way of honouring the person named in the book and acknowledging that all revelation was from the same ultimate source — God. Since Moses was the great lawgiver, all laws ultimately came to be attributed to him, even if they were written much later. Solomon was thus credited with many of the wisdom writings. In the same way letters from the early Christian era were attributed to Paul and the other apostles.

Canonization

Some of the written materials were gathered into collections and came to assume a prominent role in community life. As they became more important, people were more hesitant to change or alter them while copying. They began to look on these books as "inspired," which means "God-breathed." They ceased being a part of an ongoing process of revision and became fixed as the scripture of the community. Careful techniques were developed to prevent mistakes being made in copying.

The crucial steps in this process seem to have happened in response to specific historical events that called for strong responses. For the Jewish Bible (which Christians have called the Old Testament or Older Testament), this process began during the time of the Kings when there were political struggles over the priorities of the community. The old traditions, which limited the role of the king and emphasized the equality of the people in relation to God, were under attack. The sense of crisis was intensified by the destruction of the northern Kingdom of Israel by Assyria in 721 BCE (see chapter two). In response to this crisis, some of the oral and written traditions which spoke of Israel's history were gathered and edited into a more or less coherent narrative. A collection was also made of the teachings of prophets who had drawn on these ancient traditions in warning against idolatry and social injustice.

After 587 BCE, when the southern Kingdom of Judah was conquered by Babylon and most of its leading citizens were carried into exile, these materials became even more important, and a conscious effort was made to collect and preserve them.

After the exile, as the Jewish community tried to re-establish itself under the leadership of Ezra, the first five books of the narrative of Israel's traditions, which contained most of the laws, came to be seen as the most important part of this canon. It came to be known as the Torah, which means "instruction." The historical books and prophetic books came to be known as the Prophets. A third section of the Jewish Bible, called the Writings, was finalized during the first centuries after Christ.

The exact boundaries of the Jewish Bible were therefore not fully agreed upon at the beginning of Christianity, and several books that were excluded from the Jewish Bible continued to be used by the Roman Catholic and Orthodox churches. At the time of the Reformation (fifteenth century), Protestants decided to restrict the Older Testament to the books found in the Jewish Bible. This is why there is a continuing difference between Catholic and Protestant Bibles. Many Protestant Bibles include the books that are disputed, but put them in a separate section and refer to them as the "Apocrypha." These books, however, are not an important source of conflict between Catholics and Protestants. In both Protestant and Catholic Bibles, the books are in a different order than in the Jewish Bible.

The Newer Testament was formed in a similar process to that of the Hebrew Scriptures. Because the early churches were scattered over the vast Roman Empire, and were often persecuted, communication was difficult in the first three centuries after Christ. Most of the early Christian writings were produced for individual churches, and were copied and shared when possible. So some writings would be well known in some communities but not in others. Collections were made of Paul's letters in the second century and then of the gospels. It was only towards the end of the fourth century, as Christianity was becoming an official religion of the Roman Empire, that a list of books was widely accepted as the official canon of the Newer Testament. There were several books that were widely read in the early church that were not included in the canon. There were others, like Revelation and Hebrews, that were included in spite of opposition from some communities. Writings that were believed to have been written by the first apostles were considered more important.

The Pentateuch

The Pentateuch (the first five books of the Bible) illustrates very well the complexity of the development of the Bible. Oral traditions about the origins of Israel and Judah circulated throughout the period of the Judges and early Kings. The stories of Abraham and Sarah, the song of Miriam, traditions about Moses and Aaron and Joshua were told and retold. The stories of Jacob may have circulated primarily among the northern tribes, while those of Joseph and Moses may have been better known in the south. Each tribe had its own traditions.

There appear to have been several written sources that drew on these oral traditions and other written material and that were ultimately combined into the narrative we now know. You can see the traces of these sources if you look at the way God is referred to in the first few chapters of Genesis. Chapter one consistently uses the term *Elohim*, which is usually translated as "God." But in the second chapter, God is referred to by the name *Yahweh*, which is usually translated as "LORD." (In most English translations LORD in small capitals is used to represent the Hebrew name *Yahweh*, to distinguish it from the Hebrew word *Adonai*, also translated as Lord, but without small capitals.) This difference in the way God is referred to is one of the indications that these two accounts of creation come from two different sources. To see another example of the use of sources, compare Genesis 12:10–20 with Genesis 20. Essentially, the same story is repeated but with minor differences, including the different way of referring to God.

While there are disagreements about the details of how and when these sources were developed, most scholars agree that there are four major written sources. The first, known as the Jahwist (or "J" for short) because of a consistent use of the divine name "Jahweh" (or Yahweh), was probably assembled during the time of Solomon. King David had been successful at forging a political alliance of the twelve tribes and leading the military conquest of several neighbouring peoples. The Jahwist, who some believe may have been a woman, brought together these ancient and diverse traditions, and related them to each other, probably in order to provide the new nation with a sense of unity. If Esau was Jacob's brother and Ishmael was Abraham's son, and the twelve tribes were all descendants of Jacob, then it became possible for the different tribal groups who claimed those figures as ancestors to relate to each other in peaceful ways.

The second tradition is known as the Elohist (or "E" for short) because the term "Elohim" is normally used for God. E puts strong emphasis on the "fear of God" as the attitude of obedient respect and trust in the midst of testing. It may well have come from a time of severe testing such as the mid-ninth century BCE during the struggles between King Ahab, Queen Jezebel, and the prophet Elijah, when foreign influences and the worship of foreign gods provoked great conflict within the northern Kingdom of Israel.[1]

The third tradition is known as the Deuteronomist (or "D" for short) after the book of Deuteronomy. Themes from this book also are found throughout the historical books. It is likely that these materials originated during the time just before and after the conquest of Judah and the exile. Deuteronomy describes these events as the judgement of God on Judah's lack of faithfulness to God's covenants.

The Priestly tradition (or "P" for short) was formed during the exile and emphasizes God's promise to bless Israel once again with land.

Whoever created the final form of the Pentateuch preserved much of the distinctiveness of these sources, but the final creation is much more than just a hasty patchwork. The different sources were carefully spliced and edited.

The final stage of this process is described above under "canonization."

The Gospels

Jesus did not give dictation. Nor was there a biographer who followed him around writing down what he said. Jesus belonged to an oral tradition, and his words and deeds were remembered and retold both during his lifetime and after it. Many of his parables and sayings were probably intended to have a memorable quality. But it was at least twenty to thirty years after his death that any of this material was written down. During that time, the process of telling and retelling these stories and sayings shaped the way they were remembered. Jesus' disciples thought deeply about the significance of his life and death, and, often, later ideas came to influence their memories of his life.

Some people have difficulty accepting that the stories of Jesus might have gone through this kind of development, but as one scholar put it, those who passed on the traditions of Jesus in this way were "thinkers not memorizers, disciples not reciters, people not parrots."[2]

The Gospel According to Mark was the first attempt to write a full scale account of Jesus' life and teachings. The author (who is not named, but is traditionally called Mark) lived during the war between the Jews and Rome from 66 to 70 CE. Perhaps because of that danger, and in order to help his church community understand what it meant, Mark collected many of the short stories and sayings that were circulating in his community of faith and wrote them down. The individual units often seem strung together like pearls on a string, with little relationship to each other. He arranged them into a narrative structure and added the one long narrative that had survived: the story of the last supper, arrest, trial, and execution.

Twenty or so years later, Mark's work was used as a source by the authors of the Gospel According to Matthew and the Gospel According to Luke. The use that Matthew and Luke made of Mark can be shown by placing them in parallel columns, as shown on the next page.

Matthew 3:1–10

In those days

John the Baptist appeared in the wilderness of Judea, proclaiming, "Repent, for the kingdom of heaven has come near." This is the one of whom the prophet Isaiah spoke when he said,

"The voice of one crying out in the wilderness: 'Prepare the way of the Lord, make his paths straight.'"

Now John wore clothing of camel's hair with a leather belt around his waist, and his food was locusts and wild honey.

Then the people of Jerusalem and all Judea were going out to him, and all the region along the Jordan, and they were baptized by him in the river Jordan, confessing their sins.

But when he saw many Pharisees and Sadducees coming for baptism, he said to them,
"You brood of vipers! Who warned you to flee from the wrath to come? Bear fruit worthy of repentance. Do not presume to say to yourselves, "We have Abraham as our ancestor'; for I tell you, God is able from these stones to raise up children to Abraham. Even now the ax is lying at the root of the trees; every tree therefore that does not bear good fruit is cut down and thrown into the fire.

Mark 1:1–6

The beginning of the good news of Jesus Christ, the Son of God.

As it is written in the prophet Isaiah, "See, I am sending my messenger ahead of you, who will prepare your way; the voice of one crying in the wilderness: 'Prepare the way of the Lord, make his paths straight.'"

John the baptizer appeared in the wilderness, proclaiming a baptism of repentance for the forgiveness of sins. And people from the whole Judean countryside and all the people of Jerusalem were going out to him, and were baptized by him in the river Jordan, confessing their sins. Now John was clothed with camel's hair, with a leather belt around his waist, and he ate locusts and wild honey.

Luke 3:1–14

In the fifteenth year of the reign of Emperor Tiberius, when Pontius Pilate was governor of Judea, and Herod was ruler of Galilee, and his brother Philip ruler of the region of Ituraea and Trachonitis, and Lysanias ruler of Abilene, during the high priesthood of Annas and Caiaphas, the word of God came to John son of Zechariah in the wilderness. He went into all the region around the Jordan, proclaiming a baptism of repentance for the forgiveness of sins, as it is written in the book of the words of the prophet Isaiah,

"The voice of one crying out in the wilderness: 'Prepare the way of the Lord, make his paths straight. Every valley shall be filled, and every mountain and hill shall be made low, and the crooked shall be made straight, and the rough ways made smooth; and all flesh shall see the salvation of God.'"

John said to the crowds that came out to be baptized by him,

"You brood of vipers! Who warned you to flee from the wrath to come? Bear fruits worthy of repentance. Do not begin to say to yourselves, 'We have Abraham as our ancestor'; for I tell you, God is able from these stones to raise up children to Abraham. Even now the ax is lying at the root of the trees; every tree therefore that does not bear good fruit is cut down and thrown into the fire."

Exercise

Take four different colours of pen, crayon, or highlighter and mark the passage as follows. Identify phrases or sentences that are identical or nearly identical in more than one gospel. The passages are arranged in parallel fashion to make it easier, but don't miss the rearrangements! You may need to draw arrows to identify what is identical with what.

- Yellow: mark all the material that Matthew or Luke share with Mark.

- Blue: mark all the material that is found in both Matthew and Luke, but not in Mark.

- Green: mark all the material that is found in Matthew but not in Mark or Luke.

- Red: mark all the material that is found in Luke but not in Mark or Matthew.

As you look at the material you marked with yellow, you will notice that Matthew has the same basic structure as Mark, but with slightly more condensed language, and a slight variation in the use of quotation marks in verse two. Matthew and Luke both include part of the passage from Isaiah that Mark quoted, but both eliminate a line from the prophet Malachi Mark mistakenly included in his quotation of Isaiah. Luke rearranges Mark's text more radically than Matthew and adds more of the Isaiah quotation. These features have led scholars to suggest that Mark was the first gospel written and both Matthew and Luke used Mark as a source when they wrote their gospels.

You will also notice that Matthew and Luke also include information that Mark doesn't have. Modern scholars believe that both Matthew and Luke shared another written source (which came to be known as Q, short for the German word *Quelle*, which means "source"). This is the material you coloured Blue.

Luke also has some material that neither Mark nor Matthew have included. Scholars call this material L or special Luke. This is what you marked with Red. You probably marked very little with Green, but material that is found in Matthew but not in Mark or Luke is called special Matthew or M. Did M and L come from separate written sources, from the oral tradition of the community, or is it an original composition of the authors? It may come from a variety of these sources. We don't really know.

What becomes obvious as we look at the gospels in parallel columns like this, is that both Matthew and Luke rearranged, combined, and adapted these sources in order to express their own understanding of who Jesus was and what he meant.

The three gospels can be compared this way and the lines of written tradition can be illustrated as follows:

The Gospel According to John may have had some sources in common with the others, but is a completely distinct tradition and a quite different form of gospel. It does not try to record the oral traditions of Jesus but is a literary composition in which the author expresses his theology and that of his own community by the composition of dialogues between Jesus and other figures. Once again this should not be seen as deceit, but as an attempt to express the faith that the risen Christ is alive and continues to speak through members of the faith community.

In the final stage of the process, as was noted above, these four gospels were selected from among the other gospels that had been written and became part of the canon of scripture.

Conclusion

For some, the realization that the Bible came into being through a very human, historical process is troubling. But one of the most cherished beliefs of the church is that Jesus was fully human and fully divine. If we believe this about Jesus, it should not surprise us that the Bible is just as fully human. Nor should a sense of its fully human origins detract from its significance as the Word of God, any more than the full humanity of Jesus detracts from his being the Word of God.

Review

Decide whether each statement is true or false. Check your answers against the key at the end of the chapter.

1. Most of the people in the times described in the Bible could read. TRUE ☐ FALSE ☐

2. Many of the songs, stories, and proverbs in the Bible were passed on by word of mouth for years and even centuries before being written down. TRUE ☐ FALSE ☐

3. In biblical times, written material was copied by hand. TRUE ☐ FALSE ☐

4. The authors of the writings in our Bibles often included and adapted other written sources. TRUE ☐ FALSE ☐

5. Sometimes an author would attribute a work to an ancient figure like Moses, Solomon, or Paul as a way of honouring the person to whom the work was attributed and a way of acknowledging that all revelation was from the same ultimate source — God. TRUE ☐ FALSE ☐

6. All the writings from the early church were included in the Newer Testament. TRUE ☐ FALSE ☐

7. The process of deciding which writings would be included in the Newer Testament caused many disagreements and took many centuries. TRUE ☐ FALSE ☐

Exercise on Inspiration

Most Christians agree that the Bible is inspired. The word "inspired" means "God-breathed." But there are many different understandings about what it means to say the Bible is inspired. The following are some of these ideas. Check as many answers as you think make sense.

Key: All the statements are true except for 1 and 6.

To say the Bible is inspired means:

- ☐ God was present in the events which the Bible describes

- ☐ the oral tradition faithfully described and passed on what God was doing

- ☐ those who wrote sources or books had a genuine sense of God's will in their own time and place

- ☐ the church was guided by God in selecting the materials that became part of the Bible

- ☐ God is present with the community of disciples when they read the text

- ☐ God speaks through the Bible when readers seek God's will in it

- ☐ other:

If you're beginning to get the idea that inspiration is a pretty complicated idea then you're on the right track!

Questions

1. Does the idea that the Bible has gone through a process of historical development surprise you? Does it disturb you? Does it excite you? Do you feel bewildered or intimidated? Write some of your thoughts and feelings here.

2. The fact that many parts of the Bible have been passed on and shaped by many different people and generations means that they may have been understood quite differently at different times. Might a particular text of the Bible have many possible meanings? Does this make the Bible more or less interesting for you?

3. How do you think that understanding this process of development might influence your understanding of the Bible?

Yet another way in which the Bible is interpreted is through instructional materials like Sunday school curricula. An ancient form of instructing children and adults in the faith is a series of faith questions and brief, standard answers called a catechism. Many churches encourage people to memorize a short catechism as part of their confirmation training. The section of catechism in this reading is by Martin Luther. A priest and Bible scholar, Luther led a reform movement within the Roman Catholic Church that eventually led to the formation of the Protestant churches. Among his many important teachings Luther taught that all believers, not just monks, nuns, and priests, have a vocation before God. He therefore tried to make sure that they had the opportunity to learn about the Bible as the means to faith. In *Small Catechism*, he interpreted very briefly for children and poorly educated people the meaning of the Ten Commandments, the Apostle's Creed, the Lord's Prayer, baptism, communion, and "the office of the keys."

The Lord's Prayer

Martin Luther (1483–1546)

THE INTRODUCTION

Our Father who art in heaven.

What does this mean? Here God encourages us to believe that he is truly our Father and we are his children. We therefore are to pray to him with complete confidence just as children speak to their loving father.

THE FIRST PETITION

Hallowed be Thy name.

What does this mean? God's name certainly is holy in itself, but we ask in this prayer that we may keep it holy.

When does this happen? God's name is hallowed whenever his Word is taught in its truth and purity and we as children of God live in harmony with it. Help us to do this, heavenly Father! But anyone who teaches or lives contrary to the Word of God dishonors God's name among us. Keep us from doing this, heavenly Father!

THE SECOND PETITION

Thy kingdom come.

What does this mean? God's kingdom comes indeed without our praying for it, but we ask in this prayer that it may come also to us.

When does this happen? God's kingdom comes when our heavenly Father gives us his Holy Spirit, so that by his grace we believe his holy Word and live a godly life on earth now and in heaven forever.

THE THIRD PETITION

Thy will be done on earth as it is in heaven.

What does this mean? The good and gracious will of God is surely done without our prayer, but we ask in this prayer that it may be done also among us.

When does this happen? God's will is done when he hinders and defeats every evil scheme and purpose of the devil, the world, and our sinful self, which would prevent us from keeping his name holy and would oppose the coming of his kingdom. And his will is done when he strengthens our faith and keeps us firm in his Word as long as we live. This is his gracious and good will.

THE FOURTH PETITION

Give us this day our daily bread.

What does this mean? God gives daily bread, even without our prayer, to all people, though sinful, but we ask in this prayer that he will help us to realize this and to receive our daily bread with thanks.

What is meant by "daily bread"? Daily bread includes everything needed for this life, such as food and clothing, home and property, work and income, a devoted family, an orderly community, good government, favorable weather, peace and health, a good name, and true friends and neighbors.

THE FIFTH PETITION

And forgive us our trespasses, as we forgive those who trespass against us.

What does this mean? We ask in this prayer that our Father in heaven would not hold our sins against us and because of them refuse to hear our prayer. And we pray that he would give us everything by grace, for we sin every day and deserve nothing but punishment. So we on our part will heartily forgive and gladly do good to those who sin against us.

THE SIXTH PETITION

And lead us not into temptation.

What does this mean? God tempts no one to sin, but we ask in this prayer that God would watch over us and keep us so that the devil, the world, and our sinful self may not deceive us and draw us into false belief, despair, and other great and shameful sins. And we pray that even though we are so tempted we may still win the final victory.

THE SEVENTH PETITION

But deliver us from evil.

What does this mean? We ask in this inclusive prayer that our heavenly Father would save us from every evil to body and soul, and at our last hour would mercifully take us from the troubles of this world to himself in heaven.

THE DOXOLOGY

For Thine is the kingdom and the power and the glory forever and ever. Amen.

What does "Amen" mean? Amen means *Yes, it shall be so.* We say Amen because we are certain that such petitions are pleasing to our Father in heaven and are heard by him. For he himself has commanded us to pray in this way and has promised to hear us.

Reprinted from *Small Catechism by Martin Luther in Contemporary English.*

Questions

1. What does Luther believe that prayer accomplishes? Does it actually influence God or does it only influence the person who prays? What do you think?

2. Luther stresses both the strong moral demands of God, and God's great mercy. Do you pay enough attention to each of these, or do you emphasize one more than the other?

SEVEN

SEVEN

The Strange New World of the Bible

It has been rightly said that one can justify anything from the Bible. In an argument, people on both sides of the issue may appeal to the Bible, sometimes even to the same text! Different people reading the same Bible can understand completely different things. The next two chapters explain why this happens. This one deals with the influence of world-views. The next one deals with traditions of interpretation.

Any communication involves five distinct stages, which are illustrated in the following diagram.

If I want to communicate something to you, I encode my thought in a message. The message is a set of words or symbols that are specific to my language, culture, and style of writing. The way I encode the message is the way I have learned to communicate, because of the family I grew up in, the schools I went to, the community I live in, and a host of other factors. The message must then be decoded by you if you want to understand what I mean. You will decode according to the particular experiences you have had. The more I know about you, the more helpful I can be in encoding my message. The more you know about me, the more accurate you can be in your decoding of my message. If we were talking in the same room, you could use your observations of my body language and the tone of my voice to help you interpret the message. If you weren't sure what I meant, you could ask me a question to check if you understood me correctly. Because you are only reading my words on this page, you have less information to help you decode the message.

Suppose we do not know each other well, but are having a phone conversation. If I suddenly say "Oh, I have to pick up my son now, goodbye" and hang up, you might interpret that statement in a number of ways. If you are a salesperson, you might assume that was an excuse to get off the phone. If you have young children of your own you might assume that my son is a young child who has fallen down. But if my son were an adult who was just being released from jail, you would have completely misunderstood me. If you assumed your experiences were similar to mine, you would have made a mistake. But if you were sensitive to the differences between us, you might not have jumped to that conclusion. Bruce Malina, a biblical scholar, offers a "punny" explanation of this issue:

> …what someone says and what he means to say are often quite distinct. Should you tell your girlfriend that you love the gold of her hair, do you mean that her hair will make an excellent hedge against inflation? And why would you want a hedge against inflation rather than a fence, a wall, or a stand of trees? The words we use to say and speak do in fact embody meaning, but the meaning does not come from the words. Meaning derives from the general social system of the speakers of a language. That is why what one says and what one means to say can often be quite different, especially for persons not sharing the same social system.[1]

Each person has a particular way of seeing the world that is shaped by a tremendous number of factors. This set of assumptions, beliefs, and expectations is called a *world-view*. A world-view shapes the way we see the world. Like the green glasses Dorothy wore in the Emerald City, a world-view filters what we expect and understand. This way of seeing the world will include:

- an understanding of the physical structure of the world, including ideas about whether the world is round or flat, what lies beyond the geography the person inhabits, ideas about how the sun rises and sets, what the stars and moon are, the cycle of seasons, why rain falls, how plants grow, and a host of other things.

- expectations of how families work: the relationships between grandparents, parents, and children, between husbands and wives, between brothers and sisters, aunts and uncles; how people within the family relate to those outside it; whether children will do the same work as their parents; and how property and prestige will pass from one generation to another.

- expectations of how the social structure works: relationships between various classes; duties and rights in the political process; what will affect honour and prestige in the society; attitudes towards wealth and poverty.

- beliefs about what is right and wrong, good and evil; hopes and fears for the future; understandings of a person's tribe, family, or nationality, and where it came from and where it is going; religious or ritual practices, both those that are common and approved, and minority practices that may be tolerated or actively suppressed.

- a host of other beliefs and attitudes influenced by culture, economics, and family and personal characteristics.

The more differences people have, the more different their world-views will be. People in the same culture will share many of these ways of seeing the world; people of different cultures will have quite a different world-view. A traditional Chinese peasant, a Ukrainian scientist, and a Canadian farmer would differ on many of these issues. Even within cultures there are many differences. Men tend to see some things differently than women, young people see some things differently from seniors, rich people see some things differently than the poor, and so on. Personal experiences like child abuse, torture, sexual assault, a serious illness, or a tragic death may have profound influences on the way people see the world.

Developing a sensitivity to these differences will have two important implications for the way we read the Bible. First, those who wrote and assembled the Bible had very different world-views from ours. Second, those who read the Bible today will have a variety of world-views, which will often lead them to read the same text quite differently.

Recognizing the importance of world-view should help us to recognize that those who wrote and assembled the Bible would have had very different world-views from ours. It is therefore very easy to misunderstand what they were saying. In fact it would be a miracle if we didn't misunderstand them sometimes! But it is also clear that one way to avoid misunderstanding is to try to find out more about them. Our understanding will never be perfect, but by learning more about the differences between our world and theirs, some misunderstandings can be eliminated, and possibilities we had never thought of might become clear.

It is beyond the scope of this short book to provide a full analysis of the many differences between modern cultures and world-views and those of biblical times. What I can do is alert readers to be sensitive to these differences and encourage you to be open to learning more about them. The resources mentioned in chapter three will help you learn more about the historical setting and world-view of the biblical writers.

For many readers, this encounter with the radically different world-views of the Bible may raise some difficult questions. Does our sense of the importance of the Bible mean that we must adopt the world-views of the writers? It is very important to be clear about this, because many Christians throughout history have become confused by this idea. For example, because bibical writers assumed that the sun goes around the earth, the Roman Catholic Church forced Galileo to retract his conclusion that the earth rotates around the sun. Modern fundamentalists insist that because the ancient biblical writers believed that the world was created in six days, or women had to be subordinate to men, we must as well. They think that because some biblical writers believed such things, people of all time need to believe it.

While I respect the commitment of people who hold such beliefs, I do not agree with that understanding of the Bible's place in Christian life. We cannot turn the clock back two thousand or more years and try to believe everything the first Christians or the ancient Jews believed. Those who believe that we can and should do this are able to maintain this belief only by ignoring many of the differences between our world and theirs. People who ignore these differences not only fall into serious misunderstandings, but they fail to take seriously one of the central beliefs of Christian faith. As Bruce Malina puts it:

> In traditional Christian belief, Jesus of Nazareth, God's Messiah, is the concrete historical instance of the union of the divine and the human. This historical union, called

the Incarnation, took place in time and space, within a particular set of cultural norms and presuppositions. The problem with a fundamentalism that is interested only in what the Bible says — and not in what it means in terms of the social context in which it emerged — is that it implicitly denies the Incarnation. It denies the full humanity of the God-man, Jesus.[2]

The purpose of being sensitive to these differences is not so that we can abandon our own world-view and adopt theirs, but so that we can understand better what the words of the Bible meant in that long ago time. We are trying to get beyond the words of the message to the idea behind the message. The message of the Bible is what it has to say about God. And if we understand the ideas about God that the biblical writers were trying to express, we may understand more fully what God is saying to us.

But, as I pointed out earlier, differences of world-view will not just occur between ancient peoples and modern people. These differences also occur between people who live today. The more different people are, the more likely it is that they will interpret certain biblical texts differently. But this is not necessarily a bad thing. It may be that being in dialogue with people who have different understandings of the Bible can enrich our own understanding. This is particularly true of people who may be closer to the world-view of those who wrote the Bible. In reading two, "The Woman Who Decided to Break the Rules," for example, Elizabeth Amoah draws on her African heritage to try to understand the situation of the woman in the biblical story. Because her people and the Jews of Jesus' time had similar customs about menstruation, she is able to understand the story more accurately than a North American person could. In reading three, "The Salt of the Earth and the Light of the World," the people of Solentiname in Nicaragua bring their experiences as poor peasants in a military dictatorship to the reading of the Bible. Because Jesus and many of his first followers were also peasants living under Roman military occupation, the people of Solentiname may have important insights that would never occur to a middle-class citizen in a democracy. In reading seven, which follows this chapter, a woman from the sixteenth century uses images from motherhood to explain what it means to pray "Our Father...." Such ideas might not occur naturally to men or even to some women, but they are an important reminder that God is neither male nor female, and so women's experience of motherhood can help us understand what it means to refer to God as a parent.

When we have the opportunity to encounter the perspectives of people from other places and times, they will, at times, seem unusual. It may be tempting to dismiss their insights because they are so different from our own. It is important to remember at such times that we are just as influenced by our world-view as others are by their world-views. The failure to recognize the influences that these factors have on our reading of the Bible leads to a spiritual arrogance. It is important to read the Bible, and to hear other people as they read the Bible, with an open mind.

But, as Northrop Frye once pointed out, "An open mind is a good thing, to be sure, but it should be open at both ends, like the digestive tract, with a capacity for excretion as well as intake."[3] Sometimes having an open mind can be an excuse for avoiding engagement with other people and the Bible we share. Having an open mind does not mean that we should avoid disagreement and struggle at all costs. When encountering differences, we must seek both to understand the other as fully as possible and critically examine their perspectives and ours against the text itself, to try to understand which makes more sense of the text. It may be that the other has as much to learn from you, as you have to learn from them. Such understanding and testing makes for a constructive dialogue by which we all are enriched.

The issues of world-view are challenging and complex. The strange new world of the Bible, and the strange new world that is another human being, can be threatening, even terrifying. But we need to remember that it is through such encounters that we often encounter the otherness of God. For God is the ultimate other, the one who is closer than our own breathing, and yet beyond any adequate description. In a study of encounters with the divine, Rudolf Otto wrote in *The Idea of the Holy* that such encounters always seem to evoke a combination of fascination and terror.[4] Our natural tendency is to be afraid of the unknown, the strange, the other. But if we truly want to encounter the divine, we should not expect that it will always be familiar, obvious, and comfortable.

Questions

1. Take some time to remember what experiences you have had with people of other cultures. What differences did you notice? What differences made it easy to misunderstand each other? What have you learned from them?

2. Think of a passage in the Bible that you think is strange. Spend some time looking up the words in the passage in a dictionary and reading about the passage in a commentary. See if you can figure out what is strange about that passage and how a better understanding of different cultures and world-views might help. (If you can't think of a passage on your own, you might use 1 Corinthians 8. Find out as much as you can about why the question of food sacrificed to idols was troubling to the church in Corinth.) Make notes about your plans here.

3. How might you learn more about how people of other cultures interpret the Bible? You might propose that your church host a guest speaker from another culture or a church worker who has lived with Aboriginal people. Perhaps there are resources in your church library or book store. If you can afford it, some church institutions and community groups offer study tours and cultural exchange programs. Make notes about your plans here.

With the invention of the printing press and the development of widespread literacy, the publication of books and pamphlets became another important means of interpreting the Bible. The selection that follows is from a pamphlet on the Lord's prayer by Katherina Zell, an articulate laywoman in the city of Strasbourg, in what is now France. A vigorous defender of the Reformation faith, Zell published many pamphlets and open letters to opponents and friends. She also became active in assisting the many refugees displaced by the religious conflicts raging at the time, and became a defender of the radical reformers (or Anabaptists) who were persecuted by Catholics and Protestants alike. For this she was sometimes criticized, and her husband, Matthis, who was the pastor in Strasbourg, was described as a weak man, ruled by his wife.

The Lord's Prayer

Katherina Zell (1497?–1562)

> *Our Father in heaven, hallowed be your name.*
> (Matthew 6:9)

First, I encourage you to note a little word, which belongs also to all devoted children. It is the little word Father. Note what a friendly, pleasing word it is, indeed the most blessed and comforting that one will find upon earth.… Out of great love [God] has desired to name himself a father, and especially first through Jesus Christ. For amongst the people of old, he called himself a father not often, in fact rarely, and his might went before them. But now love has burst forth and proved itself through his son, Jesus. He desired to have for him another name, even as he wished also to have another people. So too he said in the prophet: "In time I will make another covenant with them, not like I made with your fathers, but I will write my law on their hearts"….

Thus Moses and all the prophets only said, "The Lord your God", etc. which name is of the essence and dreadful, from which the people had to be in fear and awe before him. But Christ Jesus is come; he brought with him from heaven the word Father, together with the work of a father, which is his love, as John said: "God so loved the world". Therefore Christ always calls his Father in the whole Gospel.…

He also taught us to pray, Our Father in heaven, and not Our God, or Our Lord, whereby he wished to strengthen and enlarge our comfort and assurance in prayer, for no lord hears and accedes to his servant, no lady to her maid, so quickly and lovingly, as do a father and mother to their child. As our proverb says: What does not come from the heart, also doesn't get to the heart!

A woman who has never had a child, who has never struggled with nor experienced the pains of birthing and the love of the sucking infant, how will she love children in general, rejoice and share with them, as the real mother can and does. So too God, who with the people of old wished to be called not a father but a God and Lord, ... because we were fallen and disobedient to him, could show us nothing but wrath and punishment as a Lord and jealous God, for he was not experienced in the labour and hard bearing of a mother.... But the grace of God through Jesus Christ, that is the true mother, which Christ is in God and God in him. He is become our manner of human son. For this he is also named Emmanuel, that is, God with us. For he turned himself to us in our flesh, and gave us birth; with great anguish into grace, or brought us to grace. So he produced bloody sweat, as he says: My soul is in anguish even to death, and I must be baptized, that is be on the cross. How anguishing this is for me! So too ... How is my soul deeply troubled. What shall I say? Father help me out of this hour? But I am come for this hour! And he gives the parable of the labour of birth pangs, saying; When a woman gives birth, she has suffering and pain, and he refers all this to his own suffering in which he, with such effort and labour pains has borne us, given us nourishment and life, suckled us upon his breast and side with water and blood like a mother her child with her nipples. He also experienced our flesh-and-blood-ness and bore sufferings, for he had laid aside his divine essence, humbled himself, took the form of a servant, etc.... Of which the Apostle says: we have not such an high priest who does not share with us our weakness, but rather one who is tested in all points in our likeness, but without sin. Therefore let us approach with confidence the seat of grace, that is Christ Jesus, who is the true seat of grace and the mediator, and only begotten son of God whom the Father loved and has loved us in him, for through the Beloved we are all loved. For through the Son God has borne us in turn, and bore the Son from eternity. Like as a grandfather loves the child of his child, and also is his father, and the child is his heir for the reason that it was born through his child; thus God is also our father, indeed is our grandfather, and we are his heirs and descendants through Jesus Christ his son, through whom we are born again from God into new persons.

Therefore we now should cry out in trust and say, Abba, dear Father, through the children's Spirit, as we have received from Christ, which Spirit assures us that we are God's children and fellow heirs and descendants of God with Christ. As the Apostle has so beautifully taught us in Romans, and in all his letters, so also the other Apostles and John in all his writings call him nothing else than God our Father, and us dear little children. **"**

Unpublished translation by R. G. Hobbs, 1981.

Questions

1. Zell interprets the meaning of "our Father" using images of motherhood and grandparenthood as well as specifically of fatherhood. Does she bring different insights to this text than a man would, simply because she is a woman?

2. How important are our personal experiences in the way we understand a biblical text?

3. Based on her understanding of the gospel of Jesus Christ, Zell sees the term "Father" as having an intimate and generous meaning. What do you think of when you hear "Father" used of God? Are these thoughts informed more by what the Bible says about God as Father, or by your experience of your own father?

EIGHT   The Church's Book

One of my best friends is an active participant in a Pentecostal church and proudly considers himself a "fundamentalist." And even though we grew up in the same neighbourhood, attended the same schools, and have spent a lot of time together in our formative years, when we talk about issues of faith, we see many things quite differently.

For example, we often have disagreements about the roles of women and men in marriage. Much of our disagreement centres around the text in Ephesians that says: "Wives, be subject to your husbands as you are to the Lord" (Ephesians 5:22). My friend thinks that this means that husbands should always be the leaders in the family and that when disagreement persists after reasonable discussion, the husband should have the final decision. He believes that this text is clear and unambiguous and continues to be authoritative and applicable to our day. In this he is not alone. This is what his church teaches.

I, on the other hand, do not think that this text can be applied so easily to our own time. I believe that the verse that precedes it is more important: "Be subject to one another out of reverence for Christ" (Ephesians 5:21). I also appeal to other texts that indicate that the basic thrust of the gospel is not to maintain patriarchal sexual roles, but to challenge them: "There is no longer Jew or Greek, there is no longer slave or free, there is no longer male and female; for all of you are one in Christ Jesus" (Galatians 3:28). Also, I believe that Ephesians 5:22 cannot be correctly understood without considering how it would have been understood by those who first read it, and I think that they would have understood it quite differently than my friend does. For these and other reasons, I do not agree with my friend about how he reads these words. And in that I am not alone. This is what my church teaches.

When my friend and I disagree, it is not just the private opinions of two individuals that are clashing. The conflict between us is the difference between the ways our two communities of faith read the Bible. Each of us reads the Bible as a part of a community of faith with a particular tradition of interpretation. We read as we have been taught to read, and we interpret as we have learned to interpret. My friend and I belong to quite different traditions of interpretation, and so we read the Bible quite differently. This is because the Bible is not a book that people read primarily for private enjoyment, but the book of a particular community. The Bible emerged out of the life of the church and ever since has shaped the beliefs and practices of the church.

Before the invention of the printing press in about 1440 CE, books had to be copied by hand. As a result they were very expensive, and it was only very wealthy individuals who could afford to own any book, let alone a book as thick as the Bible. So most Bibles would have been owned by a community of faith, rather than an individual. And it would have been read, not by individuals sitting alone, but as part of the community's worship and study. The Bible is therefore, first and foremost, the book of a community of faith. It was assembled primarily to reinforce and preserve the beliefs and practices of the church.

The invention of the printing press has made the Bible available and inexpensive. This has made it possible for people to read it alone. But the book never stands alone. It is always read and interpreted as part of a tradition that helps people understand what is important and what is not important, how the different parts relate to each other, and how the words in the text are to be lived out in the lives of the community and the individuals it comprises.

Many people have a quite negative understanding of tradition. They see tradition as the dead weight of the past that prevents anything new from being thought or done. But that is not the way that I am using the word. For me, tradition is neither positive nor negative, but simply a reality of the way we live. Each of us learns to speak as part of a tradition of language. Scientific research and the formation of theories occur within a tradition of inquiry called "physics" or "chemistry." All human activities are carried on as part of a tradition. And traditions are not necessarily unchanging or uniform. One way of defining a tradition is to describe it as a community engaged in argument that goes on for generations.[1] In other words, a tradition can incorporate a variety of different voices, all participating in a lively discussion.

Another way of thinking about tradition is to compare it to a river, with twists and bends, eddies and currents. If you have ever been swimming, rafting, or canoeing in a river you will know that the river is constantly moving and changing. At different places in the river the water will be moving in quite different directions and at different speeds.

Like rivers, neither churches nor traditions of biblical interpretation are unchanging nor uniform. They are dynamic, evolving, and complex. The way that we read the Bible today is quite different than the way it was read a hundred or a thousand years ago. And just as churches are made up of a variety of people, so traditions will often have complexities and tensions within them. There are people in my denomination who are much closer to my friend's view of the Bible than to mine. There may be people in his denomination who have similar views to mine.

There are often also traditions within traditions. Within a single congregation there may be a variety of different traditions. A women's group will have its own internal tensions, but the diversity within that single group might seem minor compared to the differences they might have with another group in the church. But all of those groups will be a part of that extended argument that forms the congregation's tradition. And differences between congregations will also be a part of an extended argument that forms the tradition of a particular denomination. And the differences between denominations, like the ones between the Pentecostal Church and the United Church that emerge between my friend and me, are all currents within the broad river that is Christianity. So traditions are often layered within traditions.

Usually some of the currents within a tradition will be more powerful and dominant than others. This may be because of the number of people who are committed to them, and because of the power and wealth those people hold. The perspectives and traditions that belong to small, poor, powerless groups will be relatively invisible to outsiders compared to the traditions of larger, powerful, wealthy groups. But such perspectives and traditions are not less valuable or spiritually insightful because of the poverty or powerlessness of the people who hold them. In fact, I think that the Bible teaches us that it is often precisely such people who have great insights into the nature and will of God.

The Authority and Interpretation of Scripture

My own community of faith, the United Church of Canada, recently completed a careful study of how the Bible is interpreted in our denomination, in a process called *The Authority and Interpretation of*

Scripture. The process was a consultative one, beginning with the publication of a study document in 1989 that was studied and responded to by more than 1,200 groups and individuals within the United Church, and many representatives of other denominations. A final report and recommendations were received and approved by the General Council in 1992. That process itself says a lot about the way the Bible is interpreted in my denomination, for we believe that involving a variety of people in the study can help us to encounter insights we would not have otherwise discovered. In the remainder of this chapter, I want to summarize the conclusions of the final report of that process, in the hope that readers of many denominations will find it thought-provoking.

Authority

The report begins with a discussion of the authority of the Bible, acknowledging that there are several different understandings of authority. It rejects the idea that the authority of the Bible requires us to simply accept and submit to the words of the Bible. Instead the report suggests that "Authority is found in the living interaction between the written text of the Bible and the lives of believers as they are enlightened and empowered by the Spirit. We engage the text to encounter the Living Word."[2]

This understanding of authority as interactive is based on a number of observations. First, we cannot give authority to the Bible without interpreting it. "When we read or hear or say the phrase, 'the Bible says' we must remember that we are dealing with interpretation: what one reader or community understands the Bible to be saying." In order to say, "the Bible says," someone must first select a text from the Bible that they think is relevant, decide how it connects to the issue under discussion, and conclude what guidance it offers in that situation, not to mention the issues of translation that we explored in chapter three. So there are a considerable number of interpretative steps involved just in repeating the words of one translation of the Bible.

Second, there are three other authorities that the church has recognized that interact with our reading of the Bible. First, *heritage* or *tradition* is the way the Bible has been interpreted in the church's worship, teaching, and daily life. Second, *reason* or *understanding* is the application of human intelligence, science, and scholarship to questions of life and faith. Third, *experience* is the consideration of where the words of the Bible connect with the life of individuals and communities, bringing "insight, empowerment, and conviction." These three authorities, along with the Bible, are all important resources in addressing questions of discipleship. The Bible doesn't stand alone; it always interacts with the other authorities. These authorities are usually referred to as the Wesleyan Quadrilateral, because they were formulated by John Wesley, the founder of the Methodist Church.

Given this interactive understanding of authority, and in "keeping with our scriptural interpretations, the best features of our heritage, the insights of our understanding and the encounters with God in our experience" the church adopted the following standards of evaluation for any claim to authority in the life and work of The United Church of Canada:

- **God's historic self-revelation in Jesus Christ is crucial in establishing what has legitimate authority in Christian community.** This self-revelation "is the lens through which we must see and the scale by which we must weigh anything that claims authority in relation to us. That includes potentially conflicting passages of Scripture."

- **Legitimate authority, in every case, enhances community of the whole created earth.** This acknowledges the importance of the vision of a just and loving community throughout the Bible, and especially in Jesus' teaching about the Kingdom of God.

- **The word of God, in every case, is larger than the text of the Bible.** According to John's gospel the "word of God" is Jesus Christ. As I suggested in chapter one, the Bible consists of witnesses to the living God. "Our challenge and our call, therefore, is to recognize in the biblical text the signposts which point us to the Living Word of God. This Word, while related to the text, draws us beyond it to the faithful pilgrimage of daily living."

Convictions

In addition to these conclusions about the nature of authority, the report proposed a number of convictions to express our understanding of the Bible in our church. Each conviction is in the form of a statement of faith about how God is calling us to interact with or "engage" the Bible.

- **God calls us to engage the Bible as foundational authority as we seek to live the Christian life.** "Scripture shapes us as a community of God's people. We turn to it in our struggle to understand God's convicting, liberating and transforming Word for us today and to pass on the story to subsequent generations. And in this activity, we can observe the ongoing working of God's Spirit with the people of God."

- **God calls us to engage the Bible as a church seeking God's community with all people, living creatures, and the earth.** "God calls us to live in communities of love and justice. More and more, we must recognize that we are shaped by our communities and that, if our faithfulness is to be complete, a major component of our God-given communities must be God's creation, including all living creatures and the earth."

- **God calls us to engage the Bible to experience the liberating and transforming Word of God.** "Liberation is the power of God to free us from those forces that oppress and estrange us from God, God's community and God's creation. Transformation is the activity of grace within us that changes individuals and communities.... In the dominant western Christian tradition, [liberation and transformation] have generally been understood to be liberation from individual sin and death and a transformation to a new way of life. Today we need to affirm different streams within this dominant tradition as well as other traditions that have understood sin as a social condition. Often Christians have been part of those systems and structures experienced by others as oppressive. The call to liberation and transformation comes to both the powerless and the powerful and, always, the liberation of the former is linked to the transformation of the latter."

- **God calls us to engage the Bible with an awareness of our theological, social, and cultural assumptions.** This is the issue of world-view that I explored in chapter seven. "Our understanding of scripture is filtered through our assumptions. Having assumptions is neither right nor wrong, it is simply a function of being human…. Listening to others and examining our assumptions in the light of theirs brings us to a new understanding and appreciation of both. When we truly enter into conversation with others, we know that we risk being changed by the power of God's Spirit. In such an interchange we seek not to break the spirit of others but to honour and respect them, even while inviting them to join us in responding to God's invitation to liberation and transformation."

- **God calls us to engage the Bible with a sense of sacred mystery and in dynamic interaction with human experience, understanding and heritage.** "When engaging scripture, we walk on holy ground. Thus, as we engage the scriptures, awe and wonder should set the tone of our involvement. It is a mystery as well, that, through human experience, understanding and heritage, we can gain further insight into God's word…. Always however, we must seek to be attentive to that which is outside our human sources, to the sacred mystery which lies beyond experience, understanding and heritage."

- **God calls us to engage the Bible trusting God's Spirit to enliven our understanding and to empower our acting.** "The Spirit who breathed life-giving air into the nostrils of humanity has also breathed life-giving power into both the writing and the engaging of Scripture. As we engage scripture, that same Spirit can bring us life-giving understanding…. We trust in the Spirit's presence as we work together to discern the meaning of scripture for our faith and action in the world."

Insights and Implications

A final section of the report explores what effect this study should have on the life of the United Church as a whole and the congregations that comprise it. It makes suggestions in five major areas:

- **Engaging the Bible is not an option for the Christian community.** Given the importance of the Bible to the whole church (not just to ministers), it is important to consider ways in which the church can make the Bible more central to its decision making, and equip participants to integrate the biblical story into their own life stories.

- **When we engage the Bible, individually and collectively, we are deeply influenced by and entangled in the world-views of the particular nation/community/family in which we live.** Because the way we read the Bible is influenced by who we are, it is important for us to become more aware of some of the diverse perspectives within our congregations and wider church that affect our reading of scripture. This is one of the reasons I have included the readings from different places and times in this book.

- **Our interpretation of scripture is most clearly shown in the way we live.** If the way we engage the Bible is to be faithful to God's Word, it must not be used as an instrument of domination but of liberation. To live in a way consistent with the liberating word of the Bible, we must consider the implications of our reading for the poor, for women, for minorities, and try to find ways of hearing the views of such people as part of our engagement with scripture.

- **Interpretation is unavoidable when we are engaging the Bible.** Congregations need to be more intentional about helping people recognize the diversity of interpretations, and the various methods of interpretation that give rise to different interpretations.

- **Each interpretation is an invitation to ever new discoveries and insights into God's covenant with life and the earth.** We do not engage the Bible simply to have old ideas and viewpoints confirmed. Engaging scripture requires a willingness to be open to the otherness of God, which may sometimes come through encountering people of different opinions and viewpoints.

This statement by The United Church of Canada is not intended to be descriptive of the way all United Church people read the Bible. My church is a very diverse one, and not everyone reads the Bible this way. The statement is, however, intended to offer guidance about the kind of things we should be thinking about as we read the Bible.

Conclusion

We have learned that our reading of the Bible is influenced by world-view and church tradition. This means that there will be significant differences between the way that people from different cultures and denominations interpret the Bible. While such differences have led to violent conflicts in the past, however, they are not always negative, nor do they mean that we cannot respect and work with those with whom we have differences. As I pointed out in chapter seven, differences of this kind can be positive.

Perhaps the Bible itself can give us a hint of how to deal with this. In 1 Corinthians 12 and other places, Paul speaks of some differences as gifts of the Spirit. The church is like a body made up of many different parts, each of which contributes something to the whole. Differences between believers are to be thought of as gifts to be cherished, not problems to be eliminated. It may be that different churches and cultures can also be seen as gifts of the Spirit, reminders that no one church has the whole truth, and that no one culture is perfect. It may be that we need to think of some diversity as the gift of God to be explored and cherished.

In this century, most of the major churches have joined interchurch organizations, the largest of which is the World Council of Churches. National organizations like the Canadian Council of Churches and the National Council of Churches in the United States have also been formed. These councils provide forums for churches to talk together, learn from each other, and co-operate on a variety of different goals. They also serve as a reminder to all involved that Christianity is bigger than one denomination, and that our differences may witness in different ways to the glory of God.

Sometimes, however, our differences cannot be considered gifts, but have to be seen as distortions of Christian faith. I believe that my friend's defence of patriarchal authority is such a distortion. There are at least two other modern examples of such situations. The first came during the Nazi era in Germany, when the German church was co-opted by Nazi sympathizers who considered Hitler a new Moses. Those who opposed this development formed the Confessing Church. The second was during the apartheid era in South Africa. The white Dutch Reformed Church of South Africa believed that apartheid could be justified biblically, on the basis of Older Testament passages that called on Israel to keep itself separate from other nations. This was a view that was not shared by the other members of the World Alliance of Reformed Churches, which declared apartheid a heresy and expelled the Dutch Reformed Church. Eventually that Church realized its error and renounced its support of apartheid.

We all read the Bible through the eyeglasses of a tradition. We cannot avoid that. What we can and must do is test the tradition against the original message. Often we will find that our traditions are faithful developments of Jesus' teaching, even if they diverge from one another. But sometimes, we will find that traditions are not developments of Jesus' message, but contradictions of it. And in that case we must voice our dissent quite strongly. In such situations it is helpful to have inter-denominational organizations in which conversation and dialogue can take place, and we can test our own perceptions to make sure that we are not just being narrow-minded.

Exercises

1. Remember encounters that you have had with people who interpret the Bible quite differently from you. How much of the difference is due to different traditions of interpretation and how much to personal insight?

2. What kind of differences can you identify within your own congregation or denomination? Do you see these differences as enriching your community or destructive to it?

3. If you are a member of the United Church of Canada, read again carefully the summary of *The Authority and Interpretation of Scripture* in this chapter. Ask to what extent the report describes your own experience within the church. Where does the report challenge you to look at things differently? If you are a participant in another denomination, find out as much as you can about how your tradition interprets the Bible. How is this different than what you have read in this chapter? Make notes about your plans here.

4. Find out as much as you can about the tradition of a neighbour or a friend. Compare this with your own tradition. What are the differences? How do those differences affect our understanding of the Bible? Make notes about your plans here.

Clement lived in Alexandria, Egypt, in what was then one of the great cities of the world, a centre of culture, scholarship, power, and wealth. It also had a strong community of what came to be called Christian Gnostics, a group that believed that all physical things, including material possessions, were evil, and that Christ came to rescue us from this physical world. They taught that those who wanted to be spiritually mature needed to free themselves from concern with all material possessions. Clement opposed this tendency with the teaching that God's creation was good, and that the evil is not in physical things themselves, but the use we make of them. In this sermon, he interprets the story of the rich young man in Mark 10:17–31, who is told to give away everything he has, and so turns sorrowfully away. You may find the language of this sermon a little difficult, because the translation was done about a century ago.

The Rich Man's Salvation

Clement of Alexandria (CE 150–220)

Perhaps the reason of salvation appearing more difficult to the rich than to poor men, is not single but manifold. For some, merely hearing, and that in an off-hand way, the utterance of the Savior, "that it is easier for a camel to go through the eye of a needle than for a rich man to enter into the kingdom of heaven," despair of themselves as not destined to live, surrender all to the world, cling to the present life as if it alone was left to them, and so diverge more from the way to the life to come, no longer inquiring either whom the Lord and Master calls rich, or how that which is impossible to man becomes possible to God. But others rightly and adequately comprehend this, but attaching slight importance to the works which tend to salvation, do not make the requisite preparation for attaining to the objects of their hope....

What then was it which persuaded [the rich young ruler] to flight, and made him depart from the Master, from the entreaty, the hope, the life, previously pursued with ardour — "Sell thy possessions." And what is this? He does not, as some conceive off-hand, bid him throw away the substance he possessed, and abandon his property; but bids him banish from his soul his notions about wealth, his excitement and morbid feeling about it, the anxieties, which are the thorns of existence, which choke the seed of life....

What peculiar thing is it that the new creature the Son of God intimates and teaches? It is not the outward act which others have done, but something else indicated by it, greater, more godlike, more perfect, the stripping off of the passions from the soul itself and from the disposition, and the cutting up by the roots and casting out of what is alien to the mind. For this is the lesson peculiar to the believer, and the instruction worthy of the Savior. For those who formerly despised external things relinquished and squandered their property, but the passions of the soul, I believe, they intensified. For they indulged in arrogance, pretension, and vainglory, and in contempt of the rest of mankind, as if they had done something superhuman. How then would the Savior have enjoined on those destined to live forever what was injurious and hurtful with reference to the life which He promised? For although such is the case, one, after ridding himself of the burden of wealth, may none the less have still the lust and desire for money innate and living; and may have abandoned the use of it, but being at once destitute of and desiring what he spent, may doubly grieve both on account of the absence of attendance, and the presence of regret. For it is impossible and inconceivable that those in want of the necessaries of life should not be harassed in mind, and hindered from better things in the endeavor to provide them somehow, and from some source....

And how much more beneficial the opposite case, for a man, through possessing a competency, both not himself to be in straits about money, and also to give assistance to those to whom it is requisite so to do! For if no one had anything, what room would be left among men for giving? And how can this dogma fail to be found plainly opposed to and conflicting with many other excellent teachings of the Lord? "Make to yourselves friends of the mammon of unrighteousness, that when we fail, they may receive you into the everlasting habitations" [Luke 16:9]. "Acquire treasures in heaven, where neither moth nor rust destroys, nor thieves break through" [Matthew 6:19]. How could one give food to the hungry, and drink to the thirsty, clothe the naked, and shelter the houseless, for not doing which He threatens with fire and the outer darkness, if each man first divested himself of all these things? Nay, He bids Zaccheus and Matthew, the rich tax-gatherers, entertain Him hospitably. And He does not bid them part with their property, but, applying the just and removing the unjust judgment, He subjoins, "To-day salvation has come to this house, forasmuch as he also is a son of Abraham" [Luke 19:9]. He so praises the use of property as to enjoin, along with this addition, the giving a share of it, to give drink to the thirsty, bread to the hungry, to take the houseless in, and clothe the naked. But if it is not possible to supply those needs without substance, and He bids people abandon their substance, what else would the Lord be doing than exhorting to give and not to give the same things, to feed and not to feed, to take in and to shut out, to share and not to share which were the most irrational of all things?...

Riches, then, which benefit also our neighbours, are not to be thrown away. For they are possessions, inasmuch as they are possessed, and goods, inasmuch as they are useful and provided by God for the use of men; and they lie to our hand, and are put under our power, as material and instruments which are for good use to those who know the instrument. If you use it skillfully, it is skillful; if you are deficient in skill, it is affected by your want of skill, being itself destitute of blame. Such an instrument is wealth. Are you able to make a right use of it? It is subservient to righteousness. Does one make a wrong use of it? It is, on the other hand, a minister of wrong. For its nature is to be subservient not to rule. That then which of itself has neither good nor evil, being blameless, ought not to be blamed; but that which has the power of using it well and ill, by reason of its possessing voluntary choice. And this is the mind and judgment of man, which has freedom in itself and self-determination in the treatment of what is assigned to it. So let no man destroy wealth, rather than the passions of the soul, which are incompatible with the better use of wealth. So that, becoming virtuous and good, he may be able to make a good use of these riches. The renunciation, then, and selling of all possessions, is to be understood as spoken of the passions of the soul....

And that [soul] is unclean which is rich in lusts, and is in the throes of many worldly affections. For he who holds possessions, and gold, and silver, and houses, as the gifts of God; and ministers from them to the God who gives them for the salvation of men; and knows that he possesses them more for the sake of the brethren than his own; and is superior to the possession of them, not the slave of the things he possesses; and does not carry them about in his soul, nor bind and circumscribe his life within them, but is ever labouring at some good and divine work, even should he be necessarily some time or other deprived of them, is able with cheerful mind to bear their removal equally with their abundance. This is he who is blessed by the Lord, and called poor in spirit, a meet heir of the kingdom of heaven, not one who could not live rich....

The point of the parable is evident. Let it teach the prosperous that they are not to neglect their own salvation, as if they had been already foredoomed, nor, on the other hand, to cast wealth into the sea, or condemn it as a traitor and an enemy to life, but learn in what way and how to use wealth and obtain life.

From *The Ante-Nicene Fathers*, vol. II. (New York: Charles Scribner's Sons, 1926)

Questions

1. Clement's interpretation of this passage has become part of many traditions of interpretation. For this reason, when I first read it, it sounded familiar. Did it sound familiar to you? If so, where have you heard it before? If not, how have you been taught to understand this passage?

2. Clement teaches that the issue of wealth and poverty is primarily the concern of the individual and his or her own relationship with God. I think that wealth and poverty is also an issue of community life, for wealth and poverty create divisions and ranks. My opinion is influenced by other traditions of interpretation. Are we just different, or is there a way of deciding which of us is right?

3. Clement assumes that the audience of his sermon is wealthy. Is that your situation? What, if anything, does the story of the rich young ruler say about your own relationship with money? How does the story, and Clement's use of it, challenge you?

The Bible and Modern Life

NINE

The Swiss theologian Karl Barth said earlier in this century that Christians should live with the Bible in one hand and the newspaper in the other. He wanted people to turn from the issues of their daily lives and societies to the Bible, and from the Bible back to daily life. That brings us back to the reason we wanted to read the Bible in the first place: so that we learn how to live as Jesus' disciples. A disciple is a student or follower and discipleship is the way we seek to follow Jesus. Just like the ancient disciples, we want to learn who God is and what it means to live in relationship with God.

For Christians, reading the Bible is never a goal in and of itself. It is a means to an end. By reading the Bible we become a part of the story of God's people that began with Abraham and will go on for centuries to come. By understanding as fully as possible the ancient witnesses to God whose testimony is preserved in the Bible, we are helped to understand what it means to live out that story in our own lives. The way we live out that story will not be the same as the way that the biblical witnesses did. Because our times are different, God is calling us to different responses. But God is the same, and the ancient witnesses can help us to see who God is and what God is doing in our lives and our time.

So the last step in developing biblical literacy is the most important, and requires the most creativity. We cannot avoid the earlier steps that help us to encounter those ancient witnesses, but the purpose of those steps is to return us to the present so that we can discern God's presence and calling in our own lives.

The Bible influences our lives in three major ways: through the Bible's influence on the church, its effect on our character, and its influence on our specific decisions. First, the church is shaped by its encounter with the Bible. The rituals, teaching, and practices of the church are largely efforts to enact and live out the meaning of the Bible. Participants in a community of faith are affected indirectly by the Bible's influence on the church. For example, the Bible stresses the importance of sharing our wealth with those who are less fortunate, and supporting those who are called to special ministries within the church. This has led to the practice of making an offering in each service of worship. The offering, in turn, keeps the importance of generous giving at the very centre of the church's life. The practice of making an offering shapes the character of church participants and helps to make them more generous, less selfish people. Statistics show that people who are active participants in churches also contribute, on average, significantly more to other charities than do people who are not church members. The church helps to shape the character of participants by its living out of its understanding of the Bible.

And so the second way in which the Bible affects us is through its influence on our characters. Generosity is a quality of character, not an isolated choice; generous people are predisposed to give of their time, energy, money, and property to assist those around them. Generosity, courage, faithfulness, and wisdom are all qualities of character, which give rise to specific patterns or habits of behaviour. This is not a question of behaving in a certain way, but of being a particular kind of person. We do not choose in every case to be generous, brave, faithful, or wise, but because we are a certain kind of people, we act habitually in certain ways. In Jesus' parable of the judgement of the sheep and the goats (Matthew 25:31–46), the judgement turns not on a specific incident of helping a needy neighbour, but on habits of generosity or lack of generosity.

Character includes, among other things, issues of faith, perception, attitudes, and intentions. Faith refers to what we place our trust in and what we are loyal to. Most of us place faith in many things: our family members, friends, income, cultural heroes, nations, and various causes, to name just a few. Sometimes our faith is well placed and sometimes it is not. The first of the Ten Commandments addresses the question of what our ultimate faith and loyalty is given to: "You shall have no other gods before me." Anything that we put our faith and trust in can be understood as a god. So the commandment does not forbid us from putting faith in other things besides God, but it warns us that if there is conflict, faith in God must come first, so we will have a way of deciding rightly. An employee, for example, may place significant faith in his or her job and income, but if a boss orders the employee to do something illegal or unethical, then the employee will face a conflict of allegiance. In such a case, it makes a big difference whether the person places faith and trust in God.

What we perceive as important is what we pay attention to, and this profoundly influences how we act. In Jesus' story of the rich man and Lazarus (Luke 16:19–31), the rich man enjoyed good food and fine wine, and did not even seem to see the starving begger outside his door. Because he did not think the beggar was important, he did not pay attention to this neighbour whom God required him to love.

Attitudes are other habits of thought that shape the way we respond to various situations. Are we optimists or pessimists, spiteful or compassionate? Self-esteem is an attitude. Do we habitually think of ourselves as important and worthwhile or unimportant and unworthy? Jesus once said that it is not what goes into our mouths that defiles us — what we eat passes through us and is eliminated. But what comes out of our mouths comes from the heart and reveals the inner attitudes of envy and greed that motivate evil behaviour (Matthew 15:10–20). Gratitude, generosity, patience, and humility are among the attitudes that are fostered by Christian faith.

Intentions are goals, what we try to achieve. Most of us have a sense of what our lives are for, or what we think is important. Some people live very much in the moment, seek only to enjoy the present. Others seek to gain wealth, prestige or material possessions for themselves. Other people desire education or self-improvement. Still others devote themselves to their children or the betterment of the whole society. Jesus encouraged his followers to shape their intentions in a specific direction: "Strive first for the kingdom of God and God's righteousness and all these things will be given to you as well" (Matthew 6:33).

These elements of character are shaped by our communities and the stories or narratives that tell us what our lives are for and what good people are like. For Christians, the stories of Israel, Jesus, and the early church shape our characters. By putting our faith in the God made known through Jesus, seeking to perceive what God wants us to perceive, developing attitudes of generosity, faithfulness, hope, and love, and seeking the goal of God's reign, we develop the kind of character that God desires for us all.

The third way in which the Bible affects our lives is by its influence on specific decisions that we have to make. The question of how the Bible should influence specific decisions is not an easy one. It involves questions of which biblical texts are relevant, what they mean, and how they relate to each other. Such questions presume that the person making the decision knows the Bible and how to read it; in short, that the person has been formed as a person of Christian character as part of a tradition of interpretation. In other words, only a person who has been influenced by the Bible in the first two ways can really use the Bible in the third way. It is therefore probably less important to be able to quote chapter and verse from memory than it is to become biblical people.

The ability to integrate our reading of the Bible into our lives does not happen by accident. It requires us to develop regular practices of reading the Bible and exploring the issues of modern life, and to preserve space in our lives for integrating them. The work of integrating the two is known as "theology." Theology is formed from the two Greek words *logos* (word) and *theos* (God), and literally means "words about God" or "thinking about God." Many people think of theology as something that professors and scholars do, but in fact, theology is something that anyone who thinks about God and how God wants us to live is practising. And the more carefully you do that thinking, the better a theologian you will be.

Theology, however, is not primarily an intellectual exercise, but one that helps us think carefully about discipleship. Discipleship is the practice of seeking to live as God wants us to live. So theology only fulfills its purpose when it helps us to make the transition from thinking about God to living the way we believe God wants us to live. Jesus once told a story about a man who worked very hard storing enough food so that he could retire. But before he had a chance to retire, he died, and all his effort in storing that food went to waste (Luke 12:16–20). The same thing can be true of theology. Theology is useless if it gets stored as knowledge but does not get put to work. Discipleship means putting theological thinking to work.

It would be a mistake, however, to think of theology only as the effort to move from the Bible to discipleship. Theology also moves in the other direction, from the questions and issues which arise in our discipleship, to the Bible. Theology is a two-way process as the written text of the Bible is brought into the context of our lives, and the two inform each other.

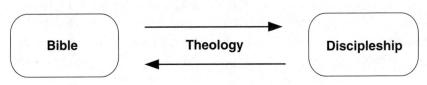

The readings and teachings of other theologians can be very useful in helping us to learn about the Bible and how other people in various times and places have interpreted the Bible and put its teachings into practice, but the ultimate test of theology is not how much we know, but what we do with what we know. Discipleship can never be read from a book, but is always a creative encounter with a living God. That means that your discipleship will not be exactly like anyone else's. Christianity is not a cult in which individuals turn over the responsibility for their discipleship to a powerful leader. The freedom of Christianity is a freedom to respond to your own very personal call, the path that you believe that God is calling you to walk.

This call is personal, but there are some common elements to it. First, while it is personal, it is also communal. It is a call to exercise your discipleship within a community of other people who are also seeking to live out their own personal discipleship, and who can support, encourage, and challenge each other in the living of that discipleship. That is why participation in a community of faith or a congregation is so important.

Second, it is a call to ministry. Just as many of us think of theologians as "someone else," we also tend to think of ministers as "someone else." Ministry, however, simply means "service," which is something that every disciple is called to. There is a story about three stonemasons who were helping to build a cathedral. Someone asked each of them what they were doing. One said, "I am putting one stone on another in order to build a wall." The second replied, "I am working so that I can purchase food and clothing for myself and my family." The third had this response: "I am building a house of God so that people may come and worship and be joyful."[1] Like those stonemasons, we can think of the various forms of work we do, as just putting one stone on another, or as something we have to do to satisfy other goals. Or we can see them as a way of serving God and our neighbours. It is this last way of looking at the activities of our lives that transforms them into ministries.

In the first letter of Peter, these words are addressed to all Christians: "But you are a chosen race, a royal priesthood, a holy nation, God's own people, in order that you may proclaim the mighty acts of [God] who called you out of darkness into [God's] marvelous light" (1 Peter 2:9). That passage makes it clear that the priesthood or ministry belongs to everybody. In a passage in Ephesians, it is clear that the work of ordained and diaconal ministers is not to do ministry all by themselves, but to "equip the saints for the work of ministry, for building up of the body of Christ" (Ephesians 4:12). Throughout the Newer Testament, the word "saints" is used to refer to all the members of the church. The phrase "the body of Christ" refers to the church. So the professional minister or pastor is set apart to support the other members of the church in their ministries, so that they can build up the body of Christ. The worship, preaching, teaching, visiting, and organizing of the church in which professional ministers often have the lead role is intended to train and support the rest of the church in their ministries.

Your ministry may be your relationships with your neighbours, family members, or colleagues, or it may be a volunteer position in the church or community, or it may be your job. You may have several ministries. Your ministries are whatever you feel that God is calling you to, whatever way in which you can serve God by loving your neighbours. Your sense of what interests and abilities you have will be important in helping you discern what kind of ministry God is calling you to. If you do not have a sense of what ministry you are called to, then speak to the pastor or minister of your church, or to a trusted friend. She or he may be able to help you identify the talents and skills that God has given you and discern where those gifts can be of service to the church and community. Be careful, however! It is important that you first identify your talents and then find a place where those talents can be used. Some churches and community groups are so desperate for help that they try to fill their volunteer positions without considering the particular gifts of the people volunteering.

When you have identified the particular gifts that God has given you, are beginning to see your various activities as ministry, and are making the connections between faith and life, then you will be making good progress on the road of discipleship.

Exercise

There are three essential habits which help us to develop this last ingredient of biblical literacy. Those habits are: personal reading and meditation, small group study, and participation in a community of faith.

Personal Reading and Meditation

In chapter two we looked at patterns of regular personal Bible reading. I recommended finding a time of day when you could consistently devote fifteen minutes or half an hour to Bible reading. If you aren't doing that, or if you got started but stopped for some reason, now is the time to get started. If you are reading regularly, keep it up, but make sure you are giving yourself enough time to ask the questions that will help integrate the Bible with your life: How does my life connect with this witness? How does this witness challenge me? If I was to take the witness of this passage seriously, how would my life change?

Depending on your interests you might want to include in your personal time readings of other resources that can help you integrate faith and life. Some people subscribe to devotional magazines like *The Upper Room* or *Alive Now!*, which provide reflections for each day. Other people prefer to read resources like the *Daily Study Bible*, or a commentary suited to their level of knowledge. Still others enjoy resources that start with contemporary issues and reflect on their biblical significance. You might try alternating your personal reading and meditation time between reading a book about the Bible and reading a book about a current issue from a faith perspective. Such a practice will keep you from becoming stalled.

Make some notes about your plans here:

Small Group Study

Reading three gave an example of a small group dialogue. If you have been a part of such a group you know that discussion can bring out insights that we would not have had reading alone. Some people call this synergy. Others call it the Holy Spirit. If you have never been a part of a Bible study group, check around your church and community to see if you can find one that you can join. Alternatively, you can talk to your friends or co-workers to see if any of them would be interested in meeting with you. You will probably find that it is helpful to start such a group with a published Bible study program (see chapter three, "Study Programs").

There are so many different ideas about the Bible that it helps to have such an objective resource to get you all started on the same basis. You might want to use this book, or ask a minister or at a church bookstore for other ideas.

Participation in a Community of Faith

Becoming an active part of a community of faith is important for several reasons. First, human beings need to participate in a worshipping community. In worship we abandon the self-centredness that afflicts much of our lives and focus on God. Second, we need the support of a community of faith to live faithfully as disciples and fulfill the ministries to which we are called as God's people. Third, there is a community of faith that needs you. In our consumer-oriented world, many of us approach churches asking primarily what they can do for us. But we ought also to consider what we can do for them. Each of us has a gift that can contribute to the health and well-being of the body of Christ in our community. Finding a community of faith in which we can offer our gifts is a very big step on the road to fulfilling our ministry. Write some ideas and plans here.

Identifying Your Gifts and Ministry

Spiritual gifts are the diverse talents and abilities given by God to enrich our common life in church and community. A talent becomes a spiritual gift when we recognize it as a gift given by God for service to those around us. Such gifts are usually things that we are good at and feel good about doing. We find them fulfilling and rewarding. The spiritual gifts mentioned in the Bible are listed below. The four passages that speak most directly about these gifts are 1

Corinthians 12:4–11; Romans 12:4–8; Ephesians 4:11–13; and 1 Peter 4:8–11. Check the ones you think you have. Space is provided at the end to add gifts you don't see here.

☐ Administration — the ability to organize, motivate, and direct people to accomplish tasks

☐ Apostleship — the ability to initiate new programs or congregations

☐ Artistic Communication — ability to use drama, music, visual media, writing, etc. to communicate effectively

☐ Counselling — the ability to listen effectively and help others toward spiritual, psychological, and relational health

☐ Craft — the ability to transform raw materials into useful objects

☐ Discernment — the ability to distinguish clearly what is real and true from what is not

☐ Evangelism — the ability to communicate faith to others so that they receive it as good news

☐ Exhortation — the ability to encourage and motivate people who are discouraged

☐ Faith — a mature belief and understanding of God, ability to communicate and inspire trust

☐ Giving — the ability to support projects and organizations with gifts of money

☐ Healing — the ability to bring wholeness and health to other people

☐ Hospitality — the ability to open your home and provide food, fellowship, or shelter for people

☐ Intercession — the ability to pray regularly and persistently for people, projects, or goals

☐ Knowledge — there are many different kinds of knowledge, from technical or academic knowledge to the knowledge of people in church and community

☐ Leadership — the ability to communicate and inspire others with a vision so that they can contribute their gifts to the accomplishment of that vision

☐ Mercy — the ability to recognize others' needs and respond with compassion

☐ Prophecy — the ability to see and communicate what God wants and how God is acting in a particular situation

☐ Service — providing practical help to other people

☐ Shepherding — the ability to nurture individuals or groups so that they grow in faith

☐ Teaching — the ability to communicate knowledge, wisdom, and faith to other people

☐ Wisdom — the ability to understand situations clearly and see solutions to problems

☐ Other —

☐ Other —

Identifying your spiritual gifts will help you decide what you should be doing. But there may be several different areas of service where you could make use of your gifts. For example, the gift of administration could be used on the board of a church or in a job running a food bank. In order to decide where you are called to serve, consider what you care deeply about, what has given you satisfaction in the past, and what you think would make a real difference in your church or community.

If you want to pursue this further, consult the books listed in the "Suggestions for Further Reading" section, or ask your pastor about Spiritual Gift Inventories.

Bernard was the abbot of the Cistercian monastery in Clairvaux, France. But his abilities as both an organizer and a writer on the spiritual life brought him wide attention beyond his own community. For Bernard, prayer and leadership are not unconnected, for the love of our fellow human beings is both the prerequisite and the result of the mystical communion with God. This selection is taken from one of his major theological works, On the Love of God, written in response to an inquiry from a prominent official in the church of Rome, who asked what "the love of God" meant. It is based on the two greatest commandments: "to love God with all your heart and soul and mind" (Deuteronomy 6:5 and Matthew 22:37) and "to love your neighbour as yourself" (Leviticus 19:18 and Matthew 22:39).

On Loving God

Bernard of Clairvaux (1090–1153)

You wish me to tell you why and how God should be loved. My answer is that God himself is the reason why he is to be loved. As for how he is to be loved, there is to be no limit to that love.... There are two reasons why God should be loved for his own sake: no one can be loved more righteously and no one can be loved with greater benefit. Indeed when it is asked why God should be loved, there are two meanings possible to the question. For it can be questioned which is rather the question: whether for what merit of his or for what advantage to us is God to be loved. My answer to both questions is assuredly the same, for I can see no other reason for loving him than himself. So let us see first how he deserves our love.

God certainly deserves a lot from us since he gave himself to us when we deserved it least. Besides, what could he have given us better than himself? Hence when seeking why God should be loved, if one asks what right he has to be loved, the answer is that the main reason for loving him is "He loved us first" [1 John 4:9–10]. Surely he is worthy of being loved in return when one thinks of who loves, whom he loves, how much he loves. Is it not he whom every spirit acknowledges, saying "You are my God, for you do not need my possessions." This divine love is sincere, for it is the love of one who does not seek his own advantage. To whom is such love shown? It is written: "While we were still his enemies, he reconciled us to himself" [Romans 5:10]. Thus God loved freely, and even enemies. How much did he love? St. John answers that:

"God so loved the world that he gave his only-begotten Son" [John 3:16]. St. Paul adds: "He did not spare his only Son, but delivered him up for us" [Romans 8:32]. The Son also said of himself: "No one has greater love than he who lays down his life for his friends" [John 15:13]. Thus the righteous one deserved to be loved by the wicked, the highest and omnipotent by the weak....

II. (2.) I think that they to whom this is clear see why God ought to be loved, that is, why he merits to be loved.... For, who else gives food to all who eat, sight to all who see, and air to all who breathe? It would be foolish to want to enumerate; what I have just said cannot be counted. It suffices to point out the chief ones: bread, sun and air. I call them the chief gifts, not because they are better but because the body cannot live without them. Man's nobler gifts — dignity, knowledge, and virtue — are found in the higher part of his being, in his soul....

VII. (17.) Let us see how he is to be loved for our advantage.... God is not loved without a reward, although he should be loved without regard for one. True charity cannot be worthless, still, as "it does not seek its own advantage" [1 Corinthians 13:5], it cannot be termed mercenary. Love pertains to the will, it is not a transaction; it cannot acquire or be acquired by a pact. Moving us freely, it makes us spontaneous. True love is content with itself; it has its reward, the object of its love. Whatever you seem to love because of something else, you do not really love; you really love the end pursued and not that by which it is pursued. Paul does not evangelize in order to eat; he eats in order to evangelize; he loves the Gospel and not the food. True love merits its reward, it does not seek it. A reward is offered him who does not yet love; it is due him who loves; it is given to him who perseveres. When we have to persuade people in lesser affairs we cajole the unwilling with promises and re-wards, not those who are willing. Who would dream of offering a man a reward for doing something he wants to do? No one, for example, pays a hungry man to eat, a thirsty man to drink, or a mother to feed the child of her womb. Who would think of using prayers or prizes to remind a man to fence in his vine, to dig around his tree, or to build his own home? How much more the soul that loves God seeks no other reward than that God whom it loves. Were the soul to demand anything else, then it would certainly love that other thing and not God....

(22.) I said above that God is the reason for loving God. That is right, for he is the efficient and final cause of our love. He offers the opportunity, creates the affection, and consummates the desire. He makes, or rather is made himself lovable. He hopes to be so happily loved that he will not be loved in vain. His love prepares and rewards ours. Obligingly he leads the way; reasonably he requites us; he is our sweet hope. Rich for all who call on him, although he can give us nothing better than himself. He gave himself to merit for us; he keeps himself to be our reward; he serves himself as food for holy souls; he sold himself in ransom for captive souls. O Lord, you are so good to the soul who seeks you, what must you be to the one who finds you? More wonderful still, no one can seek you unless he has already found you. You wish to be found that you may be sought for, and sought for to be found.

Book One, Two and Seven (paragraphs 1, 2, 17, 22), pages 3-5, 19-21, 24-25, from On Loving God, by Bernard of Clairvaux, An Analytical Commentary by Emero Stiegman, Translation by Robert Walton, OSB.

Questions

1. Bernard says both that it is our duty to love God and to our benefit to love God. Why is it our duty? Why is it to our benefit?

2. He says that God is both the efficient cause (which gives the power to accomplish something) and the final cause (the reason or goal for which something is done) of our loving God. If God causes our love for God, do we have any role in that love? How can we be commanded to do something that God can only do in us?

3. What ways can you identify in your life that you love God? Do you love God for God's sake, or is God a means to another end?

Afterword

You have now been introduced to the nine ingredients of biblical literacy. In cooking, knowing the ingredients doesn't make you a great chef, but it is the first step. In reading the Bible, being biblically literate is also only the first step. It is not an end in itself, but a means of nourishing your relationship with God so that you may more faithfully live out your discipleship.

Dialogue is essential to any relationship. No relationship will survive without it. By turning and returning to the Bible again and again, we not only discover the Word of God, but increasingly we develop our own word. As we learn not only to understand the witness of the Bible, but to value our own experience and to see ourselves as part of the ongoing story of faith, we stop reading the Bible and start conversing with it. Our reading of the Bible then serves to move us in the direction of Jesus' deepest wish, that we may move from being servants, who don't understand what God wants and so must simply follow orders, to being friends, who know each other intimately and seek to anticipate each others' wishes (see John 15:15).

The heart of the biblical message is that God already knows and loves us with that kind of intimacy, and that God invites us to become his friends. It is my hope that by continually using these ingredients of biblical literacy, and developing the knowledge and experience that must accompany them, your friendship with God will grow deeper and richer, and result in the abundant life that Jesus promised.

Suggestions for Further Reading and Viewing

There is a tremendous amount of reading material on the Bible, from a wide variety of perspectives. Many of the books and resources now available in gospel bookstores come from a fundamentalist perspective that doesn't consider the issues of world-view, context, types of literature, Bible development, and other issues mentioned in this book. Much of the writing that does take these issues seriously is too technical for lay readers. Ask the salesperson at your denominational bookstore or your minister about resources for beginning students of the Bible. The works below have been selected for a reading level comparable to that found in this book, unless otherwise noted. But there is much more available than I am aware of or can list here.

Reference Works

The New Jerusalem Bible, The HarperCollins Study Bible (NRSV), and *The Oxford Annotated Bible* (NRSV) are all good study bibles with introductions, notes, and maps, but tend to be written for ministers and people trained in biblical studies. *The New International Study Bible* has a more "conservative" theological position than the others, but is easier to read for those without much training.

The Oxford Bible Atlas is available in paperback and has articles on archaeology and geography, along with maps keyed to different periods of history. *The Harper Concise Atlas of the Bible* is another useful volume.

Cruden's Concordance is a short, easy-to-use concordance available inexpensively in a variety of editions. Because concordances are based on the terms used in particular translations, you will probably want to look for one that is based on the translation you use most often. *Strong's Exhaustive Concordance* and *Young's Analytical Concordance* are larger and more technical books that include the original Greek and Hebrew terms.

The New Westminster Dictionary of the Bible is a good one-volume dictionary, but some readers may find it more than they need. *The*

Oxford Companion to the Bible is similar, but has a slightly wider range of articles. There are a variety of other Bible dictionaries ranging from small, pocketbooks to multi-volume technical works.

The New Jerome Bible Handbook is a one-volume introduction written in an accessible style. It includes articles on each book of the Bible, maps, and photographs.

Proclamation Commentaries are a series of short books that are readable, well-informed, and inexpensive. Although they are called commentaries, they are more like introductions, since they offer a general introduction to a book or group of books rather than a verse-by-verse exposition of the text.

Books

The Authority and Interpretation of Scripture (Toronto: United Church Publishing House, 1992). The Theology and Faith Committee prepared this volume to relate the convictions, passions, and strength of faith expressed in a church-wide study on the use and place of scripture in the church and to help provide directions for the future.

The Bible Makes Sense, by Walter Brueggemann (Louisville, KY: Westminster John Knox Press, 1985/Winona, MN: Saint Mary's Press, 1977) is a personal account of how and why this important biblical scholar thinks that the Bible is important. For readers looking for thoughtful insights on how biblical writings help us imagine a better world, Brueggemann's many other books are highly recommended.

The Daily Study Bible Series (Louisville, KY: Westminster John Knox Press, various dates) are readable commentaries arranged in bite-sized chunks for daily reading. The Newer Testament series is by the popular Scottish scholar William Barclay, while the Older Testament series is by a variety of authors. While I think that Barclay often misses the social and political dimensions of the biblical stories, he writes well and makes many connections to daily life.

Experiments with Bible Study, by Hans-Ruedi Weber (Geneva: World Council of Churches, 1981) is a collection of "scripts" used in settings around the world by this teacher who spent many years on the staff of the World Council of Churches. Weber's studies make use of art, drama, and fine scholarship to bring the Bible alive. Unfortunately the art work is not reproduced in the book.

The Family Story Bible (Kelowna, B.C.: Northstone Publishing, 1996), by Ralph Milton. A well-written retelling of many Bible stories for children, this book makes a special effort to include some of the neglected stories in which women are central figures. It also has the virtue of making clear that the stories are personal interpretations.

The Gospel in Solentiname, by Ernesto Cardenal (Maryknoll, New York: Orbis Books, 1982) is a four-volume set of transcripts of the Bible study sessions held in the town of Solentiname, Nicaragua. It is one of the very few resources that makes the perspective of very poor people directly available. Reading Three is from this collection.

Is This Your Idea of a Good Time, God?, by Ralph Milton (Winfield, B.C.: Wood Lake Books, 1995). Milton's book of Bible stories for adults is humorous, insightful, and provocative.

New eyes for reading: Biblical and theological reflections by women from the third world, edited by John S. Pobee and Bärbel von Wartenberg-Potter (Geneva: World Council of Churches, 1986) is a stimulating collection of writings. It is from this book that reading two was taken.

Opening the Scriptures: A Journey through the Stories and Symbols of the Bible, by George Johnston (Toronto: United Church Publishing House, 1992). This is a unique guide for the solitary reader or discussion groups. It contains illustrations, maps, charts, a guide to signs and symbols, an annotated bibliography, and index.

Rescuing the Bible from Fundamentalism, by John Shelby Spong. (Harper SanFrancisco, 1992). This provocative exploration of the Bible by a well-known American Episcopalian bishop looks deeper into biblical literacy. While the book has some major flaws (the chapter on Paul makes him sound like a guilt-ridden twentieth-century candidate for therapy), it is one of the few books written to make the fruits of scholarship available to a wider audience.

These Stones Will Shout (1975), Lord, Who are You? (1982), and *The Seventh Trumpet (1978)* are three books by Mark Link (all Allen, T: Tabor Publishing) that offer accessible introductions to the Older Testament, the gospels and the rest of the Newer Testament. They make use of poetry, story-telling, historical background, and personal experience to bring the Bible alive for people.

Transforming Bible Study: A Leader's Guide, by Walter Wink (Nashville: Abingdon Press, 1990) is an important challenge to a primarily intellectual approach to Bible study. The author provides an introduction and several examples of Bible studies that draw on the imagination and creativity of participants. (*See* the video resource section for more material from this popular teacher.)

Unexpected News: Reading the Bible with Third World Eyes, by Robert McAfee Brown (Louiville, KY: Westminster JohnPress, 1984) is a readable account of how learning from people of other cultures and experiences can help us gain new and important perspectives on Jesus' message.

Unlock your Bible, by Brian Gee (Toronto: Novalis, 1987, currently out of print). A readable overview of the biblical story.

Study Series

Serendipity (Littleton, CO: Serendipity House). The short studies contain clear directions, fun exercises, and multiple-choice questions to stimulate discussion. Each group session includes suggestions for gathering, Bible study, and caring time. Studies are available on lifestyle issues, hurt and struggle, and Bible topics.

Intersections Small Group Series (Minneapolis: Augsburg Fortress Publishers). These short studies on faith and life issues encourage an informal, friendly atmosphere for Bible study, reflection, and growth. Clear directions are provided, and leadership can be shared.

Kerygma (Pittsburgh: The Kerygma Program). Each in-depth Bible study course for groups is a guided reading of the Bible that explores scripture in its original setting and its significance for today. Preparation by participants and the leader is required.

Disciple: Becoming Disciples Through Bible Study (Nashville: Graded Press, a United Methodist curriculum house). This program is designed to develop strong Christian leaders in local churches through the in-depth study of scripture. Churches participating pay an enrolment fee and send leaders to a weekend training session.

Videos

All of these resources are available from the Audio Visual Educational Library of the United Church of Canada.

Here I Stand (1991). A series featuring interviews with speakers who represent different ways of reading the Bible.

The Prophets Speak (1989). A series exploring the prophets of the Older Testament

The RSV Project (1991). A series of interviews with scholars who explore the themes, characters, and stories of various figures in the Bible.

What about the Bible? (1991 — Part of the series *Questions of Faith III*). A variety of contemporary church leaders and writers comment on the significance of the Bible.

Whole and Forgiven (1991). A series of six experiential Bible studies based on the methods of scholar Walter Wink.

Women in the Bible (1994) and *Women in the Bible Two* (1995). Two videos in which Canadian theologian Fran Hare tells the stories of a variety of female figures from the Bible.

Notes

Chapter 1

1 Charles L. Wallis (ed.). *A Treasury of Sermon Illustrations* (New York & Nashville: Abingdon Press, 1950), 27.
2 *No Rusty Swords* (London: The Fontana Library, William Collins Sons & Company, Ltd., 1970), 313. Quoted in *The Authority and Interpretation of Scripture*, *A Statement of The United Church of Canada* (Toronto: The United Church Publishing House, 1992).

Chapter 3

1 John R. Kohlenberger III (ed.). *The Greek New Testament: UBS4 with NRSV and NIV* (Grand Rapids: Zondervan Publishing House, 1993), 102.
2 Dr. J. H. Hertz, C.H. (ed.). *The Pentateuch and Haftorahs*, 2nd ed. (London: Soncino Press, 1960), 796.

Chapter 5

1 This is the number in a Protestant Bible. In a Roman Catholic Bible such as the *Jerusalem Bible* there are an additional seven. The Apocrypha includes those seven plus a number of others. See the section on canonization in chapter three for more information.
2 Gerd Theissen. *The Shadow of the Galilean: The Quest of the Historical Jesus in Narrative Form*, trans. John Bowden (Philadelphia: Fortress Press, 1987), 79.
3 "Now my tongue, the mystery telling" and verses 1, 2, and 4 of "Thou who at thy first eucharist didst pray" are from *The Hymn Book*, (Toronto: Anglican Church of Canada and United Church of Canada, 1971), 341, 345. Verse 3 is taken from "If Such Holy Song: The Story of the Hymns." In Stanley L. Osborne *Hymn Book 1971* (Whitby: The Institute of Church Music, 1976), 345.

Chapter 6

1 This is the thesis of Hans Walter Wolff in "The Elohistic Fragments in the Pentateuch" in Walter Brueggemann and Hans Walter Wolff *The Vitality of Old Testament Traditions*, trans. Keith R. Crimm (Atlanta: John Knox Press, 1975).
2 John Dominic Crossan. *The Historical Jesus: The Life of a Mediterranean Jewish Peasant* (HarperSanFrancisco, 1991), xxxi.

Chapter 7

1 Bruce Malina. *The New Testament World: Insights from Cultural Anthropology* (Atlanta: John Knox Press, 1981), 1–2.
2 Malina, 153–4.
3 Northrop Frye. *The Great Code: The Bible and Literature* (Toronto: The Academic Press Canada, 1982), 44.
4 Rudolf Otto. *The Idea of the Holy*, 2nd ed., trans. John W. Harvey (New York: Oxford University Press, 1958).

Chapter 8

1 Alisdair MacIntyre describes a tradition as "an historically extended, socially embodied argument…" in *After Virtue*, 2nd ed. (Notre Dame, Indiana: University of Notre Dame Press, 1984), 222.
2 All the quotations in this chapter have been taken from *The Authority and Interpretation of Scripture* (Toronto: The United Church Publishing House, 1992).

Chapter 9

1 Hans-Ruedi Weber. *Salty Christians* (New York: The Seabury Press, 1963), 39.

Glossary

Because these words are all translations of Hebrew and Greek words they may vary from translation to translation. This glossary is based on the *New Revised Standard Version*. If you have a different version you may find some minor variations. Because these words were understood in different ways in different eras of history, most of them have shades of meaning that cannot be addressed in a resource of this length. For that reason, many of the descriptions below are oversimplifications. They will get you started in the right direction, but it is worthwhile to consult a dictionary and look up the word in a concordance for more information.

Angel — *Angellos* is a Greek word that means messenger. An angel usually means a messenger from God (Genesis 28:12; Luke 1:26). Sometimes, however, they are guardian angels (Matthew 18:10; Acts 12:15). In Revelation 2:1 the reference to "the angel of the church" probably has a meaning that might be described as the personality of a church. This latter sense is part of the cluster of words included below under "Principalities and Powers."

Apostle — An apostle is "one sent forth." The earliest Christians were not just passive recipients of a message, but were sent forth with a responsibility. This is true of modern Christians as well. We are both disciples and apostles (Luke 6:12–16; 1 Corinthians 15:3–11). *See also* "Disciple."

Blood — In many aboriginal cultures, the killing of an animal is accompanied by words or rituals that express a sense of respect for the animal's life and regret that the animal must die to feed the hunter. In ancient Israel, this same respect was enacted by sprinkling the blood of the animal on the ground or an altar as an peace offering for the taking of life. The blood was a symbol of the life of the animal, and drinking the blood was strictly forbidden (Deuteronomy 12:15–16, 23–25). Blood was also often used as a symbol of violent human death. The blood of Christ is a vivid way of speaking of Jesus' death (Matthew 27:4–5). Given the background of the use of the blood of an animal to atone for taking its life, it is not too surprising

that Jesus' blood came to be spoken of the same way, even if that imagery is foreign to us (Colossians 1:20 among many others). *See also* "Sacrifice."

Body of Christ — The body of Christ is an image used to describe both the bread used in the Lord's Supper (Matthew 26:26 and parallels) and the Church (1 Corinthians 12:12–27). The symbolism of communion therefore is of the Body of Christ being nourished by the Body of Christ.

Bread — Bread is often used as a symbol of all food in the Bible. It is certainly the most basic food and one of the most universal. For biblical people, bread was a reminder of the exodus, when they had to take unleavened bread because they did not have time to let the bread rise, a memory that is celebrated each year at Passover (Exodus 12:14–20). Bread was also a symbol of the blessing of God, experienced during the wilderness wanderings (Exodus 16) and so the first response of humans to bread must be to give thanks. The biblical God is a God who is concerned for the physical needs of humans, but the Bible emphasizes that physical needs are not everything (Matthew 4:3–4, Deuteronomy 8:3). Bread may also therefore be a symbol of the Word of God, and so Jesus came to be seen not only as the Word of God, but as the bread of life (John 6:25–59). Bread became a symbol of Christ's faithfulness and death, when at the last supper he took bread and said, "This is my body that is for you" (1 Corinthians 11:24).

Call — An invitation to co-operate with God in accomplishing some task. In the Bible, God calls leaders like Moses and prophets. Jesus calls disciples and apostles. In the stories about God's call, the person called can refuse and often tries, but God can be pretty persistent! (*See* Exodus 3–4; Jeremiah 1; Galatians 1:11–16)

Chosen — God chose the people Israel to be a special people. They were not chosen because they were better than anyone else or because God loves them better, but in order that, through them, God might bless the other nations. In some sense, Christians are also a chosen people. Christian faith is not a possession we have earned, but a gift that we are called to share. (*See* Genesis 12:1–3; Deuteronomy 7:7–11; John 15:16; Romans 9:4–5.)

Church — The Greek word *ecclesia* means an assembly or congregation. The word "church" can refer either to the local congregation or to the wider universal church. (*See* 1 Corinthians 1:2; Acts 20:28.)

Covenant — A covenant specifies terms for a relationship like a contract, but implies commitments which go beyond a contract. The relationship between marriage partners and family members is a covenant. The terms of care, cherishing, faithfulness, and so on may be broken, but the relationship does not automatically end when the relationship is broken. The Bible records many covenants that God made with Abraham, Noah, Moses, and David. God's relationship with Israel was often spoken of using the imagery of human covenants like marriage (*see* Isaiah 54:5–10). God's relationship with people through Christ is seen as a "new covenant" (Jeremiah 31:31–34; 1 Corinthians 11:25).

Desert/Wilderness — In the Bible the desert is the place of deprivation and testing, but also the place of purification and blessing. After the exodus, when the people were wandering through the wilderness, they experienced hunger and thirst, and through that they learned to trust God (Exodus 16:1, 17:7). After his baptism, Jesus was led *by the Spirit* into the desert to be tempted (Matthew 4:1–11). We often think of temptation as something negative, but often it serves the purpose of clarifying choices. This suggests that temptation and blessing are closely linked. That is why the Bible sometimes speaks of the tempter or devil as God's servant rather than God's adversary (Job 1:6–12).

Disciple — A disciple is "one under discipline" or a student. In the ancient world, teachers and rabbis would gather a group of students who would accompany them throughout the day and learn by example as much as direct teaching. Teaching was not confined to a particular discipline, but was related to all of life. A disciple is therefore more like an apprentice in life than a modern classroom student. In the Bible, disciple sometimes refers to the twelve (Mark 6:45) and sometimes to all Jesus' followers (Luke 6:17). *See also* "Apostle" and "Chosen."

Faith/Faithfulness — These two English words are equally valid translations of the Greek *pistis*, which means loyalty and commitment to covenants. God is faithful to these covenants (Luke 15:3–7; Romans 8:31–39). Humans are called to respond with corresponding loyalty. Belief, trust, and obedience are elements of this faithfulness. Too often people understand faith to mean only an intellectual belief in God and Jesus. Faith includes belief, but involves much more (*see* Romans 12:1–2). *See also* "Fear of God" and "Chosen"

Fear of God — A term commonly used in the wisdom literature to refer to an attitude of reverence, respect, and obedience to God (Proverbs 1:9). Such respect includes an element of holy terror before the power and majesty of God (Psalm 2:11). In many of the stories about revelations by God and angels, the first response of the human characters is that of fear, but the first words of the divine messenger are often "Be not afraid" (Luke 2:18–20).

Fire/Light — At several points in the Bible, God is portrayed as coming to people in the form of fire and light: God appears to Moses in the burning bush (Exodus 3) and as fire on Mount Sinai (Exodus 19:18, 24:17); God leads Israel through the wilderness as a pillar of smoke and fire (Exodus 13:21–22); Jesus appeared to the disciples transfigured by a cloud of light on the mount of transfiguration (Matthew 17:1–8); the Spirit comes as tongues of fire on the day of Pentecost (Acts 2:1–4). Fire and light suggest power, energy, illumination, truth, and danger that needs to be respected. God's judgement is sometimes portrayed as a purifying fire (Matthew 3:10).

God — There is little abstract speculation about God in the Bible. Rather God is the ultimately mysterious being who reveals a presence and a will to the people Israel (Exodus 3), and later through Jesus to the church (John 14:7). Although the Bible uses many images of God (eagle, cloud of light, shepherd, father, potter, mother) Israel is warned not to lose sight of God's mystery by making idols, which would restrict our understanding of God to one of these images (Exodus 20:1–6). Jesus' use of "Father" to address God has made this one of the most prominent ways of addressing God (Luke 11:2).

Gospel — Gospel literally means "good news." The good news that Jesus taught was that the kingdom of God was at hand (Mark 1:15, Matthew 11:5). After the resurrection, the early church taught that Jesus himself was the good news, as a power and presence that gave people access to God (Romans 1:16). *See also* "Salvation."

Grace — God's grace is God's generosity to people, without precondition, and quite apart from any question of whether they deserve it or not. The people Israel were chosen not because they were better than other people, but simply because of God's grace (see Deuteronomy 7:7–8). Paul speaks of salvation being by grace, which means that we are not saved by anything we do (including believing) but as a free gift (see Ephesians 2:4–10).

Heaven — Heaven is the place where God lives, while earth is the place where humans live (Matthew 6:9). The biblical idea of paradise is not the common one of people going to heaven after they die, but of the barrier between heaven and earth being broken through so that God will dwell with God's people (Revelations 21:1–4). *See also* "Kingdom of God" and "Salvation."

Hell/Sheol — In the Older Testament, Sheol is the place of the dead. It is not a place of punishment, but of waiting (Psalm 139:8). It is sometimes called the "Pit" (Psalm 28:1). In Apocalyptic writing, the experience of evil winning out over good led to a perspective that the injustices experienced in this life would be corrected in a future one. Elaborate descriptions of the torment that would be experienced by those who did evil were developed. Thus the place of the dead came to be seen as a place of reward and punishment. The term that Jesus used to describe the place of judgement, however, was *Gehenna*, the name of the place outside Jerusalem where garbage was burned (Mark 9:43–47). *See also* "Judgement."

Journey/Pilgrimage — The life of faith is often portrayed in the Bible as a journey or pilgrimage. This is especially true of Abraham, who became a nomad (Genesis 12:1–5; Hebrews 11:8–9), of Israel after the Exodus, of Jesus who wandered from place to place through much of his ministry and called his disciples to do likewise (Luke 9:57–10:12), and of Paul, who travelled constantly. A journey suggests change and new discoveries, but also unsettledness, unpredictability, and an utter reliance on God.

Judgement — Since God is just and the creator of the world, people expected that the world would reward those who lived justly and punish those who did not. But sometimes this did not happen, and so people began to hope that at some future date, God would judge the world and right the wrongs that had gone unpunished. Sometimes the expectation is that nations will be judged as a whole and sometimes it is that individuals will be judged. This hope was especially strong at times of severe political oppression. Writings that appeared at such times reflect these themes strongly (see "Apocalypse" in chapter six: Major Types of Literature). The prophet Amos pointed out that some people who saw the evil that others did and hoped for their punishment might be surprised to find themselves judged quite harshly themselves (Amos 5:18–20). Jesus condemned the hypocrisy of those who saw the speck in another's eye but failed to notice the log in their own (Matthew 7:1–5). Paul makes the wise observation that none of us is completely innocent and the best we can hope for is to purge the sinful aspects of ourselves (Romans 2:1–5). This reluctance to judge others, however, should not prevent us from being clear about what is just and right and what is not and committing ourselves to the good. There are thus a variety of understandings of judgement in the Bible that inform and correct each other. *See also* "Heaven," "Hell/Sheol," "Justify," "Righteousness," and "Salvation."

Justify/Justification — To treat someone as if he or she were just. God justifies sinners by overlooking their sins and treating them as if they were just (Romans 5:1–11). *See also* "Righteousness."

Kingdom of God/Reign of God — The term does not refer to a geographical kingdom but to a relationship between God and God's creation in which God's will is done "on earth as in heaven" (Matthew 6:10). It is not a place but a state of being in which the alienation of sin will be overcome, the world will be purified, and an intimate relationship between God and us creatures will be restored. Throughout most of the Bible the expectation is that the reign of God remains in the future, but Jesus taught that through his ministry God's reign was becoming available to people in the present (Luke 10:23–24). See also "Salvation."

Law — The Hebrew word *Torah* means both "law" and "instruction." Jewish law is never a way of earning God's favour, but is always a response to God's grace in making covenant with Israel (Exodus 20:1–2). It is instruction about how to live in covenant relationship with God. But Gentiles (non-Jews) often did not understand this, and Paul, the apostle to the Gentiles, needs to provide them with instruction about the priority of grace to law (Galatians 2:15–16).

Love — Just as there are a variety of Inuktitut words for the English "snow," there are a number of Greek terms translated into "love" in English. The term *philia* refers to the affection between friends; *philadelphia* refers to the love between brothers and sisters; and *eros* refers to erotic love, but also has a spiritual sense of the quest to possess and enjoy the divine. *Agape,* the word most frequently used in the Newer Testament, was almost unknown in Greek literature before it was used in translating the Hebrew Scriptures into Greek. Those Jewish translators may have used it because of its freedom from erotic associations, but also because it conveyed the idea of a love that sought to help rather than to possess and enjoy the loved one. It became the dominant expression used in Christian writing as well. Unlike much modern use of "love" it does not refer to a feeling, but to a choice to do good. For that reason, it is possible for Jesus to command his followers to love (Luke 10:25–28; John 15:12; 1 Corinthians 13).

Messiah/Christ — Messiah (in Hebrew) and Christ (in Greek) both mean "the anointed one." In ancient Israel, kings and high priests were anointed into office. Before the time of Jesus, the term Messiah came to refer to a person who would establish God's reign of peace. In the time of Jesus, many people expected the Messiah to be a warrior figure who would overthrow Roman rule. For Christians to believe in a crucified Messiah was a profound reinterpretation of the concept (Mark 8:27–33).

Mountains/Hills — Because Moses was understood to have received the law on Mount Sinai (also called Mount Horeb), mountains were places to meet God (Genesis 20; 1 Kings 19:8–10; Mark 9:2–8). For that reason shrines and temples were often at the top of hills or mountains. The central shrine came to be at Mount Zion, which was revered for that reason. But the practice of building shrines and temples on the tops of hills was shared by other Near Eastern religions. These other shrines (commonly called high places) are frequently condemned in the Bible, and so hills became symbols of temptation and unfaithfulness (1 Kings 12:27–33; Psalm 121:1–2).

Peace — The Hebrew word *shalom* refers not just to an absence of conflict but to the presence of right relationships among all God's people. The fullness of this peace would only come in the reign of God, so the Messiah was hailed as a bringer of peace (*see* Isaiah 9:6–7; Luke 2:14, 19:38).

Principalities/Powers/Demons — These words are strange to us. They refer primarily to forces of power that guide our world. These forces include political offices and those who hold them but also the underlying beliefs and habits that direct the person who holds the office. These powers are seen as being creations of God that have a purpose in God's world (Colossians 1:16), but that become demonic when they seek to live outside the purpose God intends for them. Sometimes these powers are seen to dwell in individuals (Mark 5:1–15). Christ has power over these powers and one of the primary meanings of Christ's death and resurrection according to Paul is that it has defeated the rebellious principalities and powers (Colossians 2:15; Ephesians 1:20–23).

Repentance — This word does not mean "to feel badly about something you have done" or "to want to change." It means the actual experience of changing. Literally it means to "turn around." Sometimes God is said to repent (Jeremiah 18:7–8). Normally, however, it is sinners who repent. John the Baptist and Jesus both teach that their followers must change in order to enter into right relationship with God (Matthew 3:1; Mark 1:15; Luke 19:1–10).

Righteousness — Righteousness does not refer to moral purity in the usual sense. To be righteous is to seek to live in right relationship. God is righteous in seeking to forgive and restore right relationship with the creation (Romans 3:21–26). People are righteous when they seek to live in right relationship with God and when they show generosity and compassion for those who are vulnerable or suffering (Job 29:11–17; Amos 5:21–24; Psalm 112:6–9; Luke 1:75; Romans 6:15–23). *See also* "Justify."

Rock — In the Hebrew Scriptures, God is often referred to as a rock, symbolizing God's faithfulness, changelessness, and protection (*see* especially Deuteronomy 32:1–43). In the Newer Testament, Christ's words are the rock on which the wise build their lives (Matthew 7:24–27) and it is Peter's faithfulness to Christ that makes him the rock on which Christ's church is to be built (Matthew 16:18).

Sabbath — The seventh day of the week on which God rested after the creation and on which Israel is to rest both as an act of religious observance and for the sake of servants, slaves, animals, and the land itself. A Sabbath year every seventh year was for the freedom of people held in slavery because of debt and to let agricultural land lie fallow. An extension of the Sabbath was the Jubilee year that was to be held every fifty years, for the forgiveness of debts and the return of lands that had been seized for default on debt. Jesus saw works of healing on the Sabbath as fulfilling the intent of Sabbath peace (Exodus 31:12–17; Leviticus 25; Matthew 12:1–14).

Sacrifice — To sacrifice is to offer something to God. There were several kinds of temple sacrifices. The sacrifice might involve grain or an animal, which might be burnt (a holocaust), or offered to God and then eaten by the worshippers (a communion sacrifice). Sometimes part of an animal might be burnt and the rest eaten. Sacrifices were offered to offer thanks, to ask for help, to seal agreements (between people, or with God — Genesis 15:9–10, 17–18), or to seek forgiveness and restore relationships (Leviticus 1–7). The prophets warned that sacrifices without righteousness were useless (Hosea 6:6). Jesus' death is described as the ultimate sacrifice that dispenses with the need for other sacrifices (1 Corinthians 5:7; Hebrews 9:26–28). The appropriate response to Jesus' sacrifice is to offer ourselves to God as a living sacrifice (Romans 12:1). *See also* "Blood."

Salvation — While this word is often understood in an other-worldly sense, its basic meaning is as a synonym for peace and the kingdom of God. Salvation refers to the state of right relationships that God desires for and with the creation. Final salvation will only be achieved in the reign of God, but whenever people seek to live according to God's will it is possible to speak of them being saved "in hope." It is unbiblical to speak of people being "saved" as if it had already been accomplished (Romans 8:24–25). *See also* "Justify" and "Righteousness."

Water — Water is a symbol of profound and diverse importance in the Bible. The land of Palestine has many dry areas that burst into life with the seasonal rains. Floods and streams of devastating force are common. Water therefore is a symbol of both life and death. The Bible holds a special regard for the Jordan River, one of the few rivers in the area that flowed all year round. Among many other references to water that had symbolic significance are the waters of creation (Genesis 1:1–10), the flood in the time of Noah (Genesis 6–9), the waters of the sea that protected the Hebrews after the Exodus by destroying the Egyptian army (Exodus 14), the water from the rock when the people were thirsty in the desert (Exodus 17:1–7), the waters of the Jordan in which Jesus was baptized (Matthew 3:13–17 and parallels), Jesus offering living water to the woman at the well (John 4:1–15), and the waters of the river of blessing that will flow from the throne of God in the new Jerusalem (Revelation 21:1–6, 22:1–2). The water of baptism carries all of this symbolism, but in addition it also refers to Christ's death and resurrection (Romans 6:3–5). Water is the symbol of drowning and destruction as well as the symbol of life and new birth. In baptism, believers experience death and new life.

Wind/Spirit —These two words are equally valid translations of a single word in both Hebrew and Greek. Whenever either word is found in the Bible, therefore, it can be replaced by the other to explore the symbolism of the passage. The wind/spirit is present at the creation and is the power by which the new creation will be established (*see* Genesis 1:2; Ezekiel 37; and Acts 2 for examples). Wind is powerful, unpredictable, uncontrollable, and invisible, all of which suggest aspects of God. After the biblical period, a full doctrine of the Holy Spirit in relation to God the Father and Christ the Son was developed by the early church.

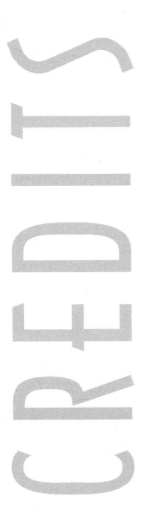